Approaches Toward Unity

Papers Presented for Discussion at Joint Meetings of Protestant Episcopal and Methodist Commissions

THE PROTESTANT EPISCOPAL JOINT COMMISSION
ON APPROACHES TO UNITY AND
THE METHODIST COMMISSION ON CHURCH UNION

SET UP, PRINTED, AND BOUND BY THE
PARTHENON PRESS, AT NASHVILLE,
TENNESSEE, UNITED STATES OF AMERICA

Dedication

O God, the Father of our Lord Jesus Christ, our only Saviour, the Prince of Peace; Give us grace seriously to lay to heart the great dangers we are in by our unhappy divisions. Take away all hatred and prejudice, and whatsoever else may hinder us from godly union and concord: that as there is but one Body and one Spirit, and one hope of our calling, one Lord, one Faith, one Baptism, one God and Father of us all, so we may be all of one heart and of one soul, united in one holy bond of truth and peace, of faith and charity, and may with one mind and one mouth glorify thee, through Jesus Christ our Lord. Amen.

Book of Common Prayer

Table of Contents

Introduction

The Membership of the Joint Commission on Approaches to Unity of the Protestant Episcopal Church, and the Commission on Unity of The Methodist Church

Introduction

Joint conversations between the Methodist Commission on Church Union and the Episcopal Church's Commission on Approaches to Unity, in which we have been privileged to serve as chairmen, have been held during the past two years. These have been encouraging and fruitful. Our commissions feel that it is important to share those fruits with the wider membership of the two Churches. In the following pages, therefore, the papers read before the joint meeting of the two commissions are published for the sake of all interested.

These papers are not meant to be official documents with which no one in the same communion as the author can take exception. In one sense, they are the work of their authors and nothing more. In another sense, they are legitimate expressions of great traditional understandings. They represent the efforts of responsible writers to explore central issues in the life of the denomination and in the Christian Faith itself, so that what ultimately results from the negotiations will have behind it a full facing of the problems in the way of unity.

From the same mother church came our two Churches, born of the same labors of history in this country's day of revolution. To England and her Church both can look in gratitude for the precious heritage of language, thought and form which still today make us more truly children of one household than our members are perhaps aware. Such kinship makes our Churches one in many sense of the word.

We are fully aware of the differences and difficulties which lie in the path to the ultimate goal of organic union. But we who have worked and prayed together in our unity commissions have been convinced that there are no insuperable obstacles to the eventual union of The Methodist Church and the Protestant Episcopal Church in the United States of America.

Because what the two commissions may accomplish can be of little value unless their thinking is shared with their respective churches, these papers are now commended to the membership of the Methodist and Protestant Episcopal Churches for study. It is our hope that a solid base of informed opinion may be laid as the members of the churches read and discuss what the commissions are reading and discussing, and that what we may do in the way of reunion will be in terms of faith even more than organization. That the members of our respective churches may be moved by the same conviction, we submit and commend these papers to their study and prayers.

STEPHEN E. KEELER   IVAN LEE HOLT

CHAPTER I

Common Historic Heritage

The Church of England

The Church of England takes its origin from earliest times. Bishops, priests and deacons from England were present at the Council of Arles in the year 314. Direct relation with the Church in Rome stems from the mission of Augustine, a Roman monk, who landed on the shores of Kent in 597. This work was united with the earlier Celtic Christianity to form the evolving Church in England and the organization of the national Church of England paralleled the growth of the English nation. This English church while clearly an integral part of western Christendom, periodically reasserted its independence from developing papal tyranny and, from time to time, the attempted tyranny of the throne. The Magna Charta (1215) was the assertion of freedom from tyranny of pope or king, as shown in its opening words: "The Church of England shall be forever free." When basic reform of belief and practice became necessary in western Christendom, the Church of England undertook its reformation, in the course of which it severed its ties with papal jurisdiction in the sixteenth century.

The Church of England holds that its ministry is in unbroken continuity through the succession of bishops, an Apostolic Succession dating from the earliest times. It has always maintained close relations with other churches making similar claims, for example, the Eastern Orthodox churches, which refused to submit to Rome and its theory of the papacy in 1054, the Church of Sweden, severing papal ties in the sixteenth century, and the Old Catholic Church of Europe which broke from Rome in 1878 when it refused to accept the new dogma of the Pope's infallibility.

During the latter part of the eighteenth century there were organized, within the Church of England, societies for special study of the Bible and prayer. Because many of these societies urged upon

9

their members a methodical use of the hours of the day, giving thus more time for bible reading, prayer and meditation, they became known as "Methodists." They were largely the work of two brothers, John and Charles Wesley, priests of the Church of England, and sons of the Church of England rector at Epworth.

The Church of England has been in the forefront of the ecumenical movement. Its Archbishop William Temple laid the groundwork for the coming into being of the World Council of Churches.

The Church of England in America

Sir Francis Drake, son of a British clergyman, brought his chaplain, Francis Fletcher, and the Church of England to the New World when, in 1579, he came ashore and claimed the new continent in the name of his Queen Elizabeth. The charters given Sir Humphrey Gilbert (1578) and Sir Walter Raleigh (1584 to 1587) provided for "public service according to the Church of England." With the dashing Captain John Smith came clergyman Robert Hunt, who at Jamestown, Virginia, in 1607, established the first permanent worship as a part of an established settlement. Captain John reported "We did hang an awning (which is an old saile) to three or four trees" and there built their rustic altar. Thus, with the settlers came the Established Church. In Boston, Kings Chapel was opened in 1689 and in 1698 Trinity Church, New York, and a chapel at Newport, Rhode Island, were consecrated.

While British colonists were settling the eastern seaboard, Spanish explorers and settlers were colonizing Florida and threatening to move north under the banner of their King and their Pope. As a buffer, England sent out General Oglethorpe to build a fort and establish a garrison at Frederica, Georgia, in 1736. As his personal secretary and chaplain, he brought Charles Wesley, and later John Wesley came to serve as chaplain to the garrison and as missionary to the Indians. In 1742 a Spanish fleet of 51 vessels moved north and landed its attacking force of 3,000 men, but in the ensuing "Battle of the Bloody Marshes" the garrison at Fort Oglethorpe completely annihilated their adversaries and ended the threat of Spanish conquest of the British colonies.

At Frederica the Wesleys established a church of their faith which today continues as Christ Church of the Protestant Episcopal denomination. As in England, the Wesley brothers organized, within this new church, a "methodist society." The Society, thus established, continues today on neighboring St. Simons Island as the Methodist Church of St. Simons.

The American revolution brought a crisis for the Church of England in America. Ministers could be ordained only in England and as part of their ordination service were required to take an oath of allegiance to the King. Understandably, many of the clergy remained loyal to their King. Some returned to England; the former established church was roughly treated. With the war won, the people of the new nation found themselves largely without the benefit of clergy. Out of this situation came into being, almost simultaneously, The Methodist Episcopal Church and The Protestant Episcopal Church.

The Methodist Church (1784)

That the people in the Societies in America were without clergy to perform the sacraments was of great concern to John Wesley. The Church of England had refused to send a bishop to America to ordain ministers. The Bishop of London even refused Wesley's personal request "to ordain a pious man" for service in America.

In 1746 Wesley had studied a book by Lord King, published in 1691, in which it was argued that in the early church there were only two orders, deacons and elders or presbyters, and that the Church of England was in error in holding that bishops were of a special "third order." For almost forty years Wesley had been studying and pondering this problem. If the thesis were correct, then he as a presbyter or priest in the true Apostolic succession of the Church of England, had the power of ordination. He ultimately came to the conclusion that "Bishops and presbyters are (essentially) one order." Acting on this finding, Wesley and James Creighton, also an ordained minister of the Church of England and others, by the laying on of hands in a service of consecration, set apart as Superintendent for the work in America, Thomas Coke, a scholarly Anglican clergyman, who held his doctor's de-

11

gree from Oxford University. This was in Bristol on September 2, 1784. Coke in turn was to go to America and ordain Francis Asbury, a lay-preacher in the Methodist Societies whom Wesley had suggested as permanent Superintendent for the work of the Societies in America. The credentials which Coke took to America were in handwriting, and read as follows:

To all to whom these Presents shall come John *Wesley,* late Fellow of *Lincoln* College in *Oxford,* Presbyter of the Church of *England* sendeth greeting:

WHEREAS many of the People in the Southern Provinces of *North America* who desire to continue under my care, and shall adhere to the Doctrines and Discipline of the Church of *England* are greatly distrest for want of Ministers to administer the Sacraments of Baptism and the Lords Supper according to the usage of the said Church. And whereas there does not appear to be any other way of Supplying them with Ministers

Know all men that I *John Wesley* think myself to be providentially called at this time to set apart some persons for the work of the ministry in *America.* And therefore under the Protection of Almighty God, and with a single eye to his glory, I have this day set apart as a superintendent, by the imposition of my hands and prayer, (being assisted by other ordained Ministers) Thomas *Coke,* Doctor of Civil Law a Presbyter of the Church of England & a man whom I judge to be well qualified for that great work. And I do hereby recommend him to all whom it may concern as a fit person to preside over the Flock of Christ. In testimony whereof I have hereunto set my hand and Seal this second day of September in the year of our Lord one thousand seven hundred and eighty four

John Wesley

Seal

On arrival in America, Dr. Coke met with Francis Asbury and other Methodist preachers (American and those sent by Wesley) in the famous Christmas Conference of 1784, held in Baltimore, at which time and place they organized the Methodist Episcopal Church. Asbury would not permit Coke to ordain him unless and until the Methodist preachers, in Conference assembled, should elect him for ordination and leadership. This they did unanimously. Then Coke, assisted by both Whatcoat and Vasey and also by Philip William Otterbein, a pietistic German Reformed minister, ordained Asbury, first as Deacon, then as Elder, and then set him apart as Superintendent. The Conference also elected Coke as

Superintendent. Asbury and Coke were at once called Bishops and all Methodist Bishops today stem from this heritage. Their succession has never been recognized by Lambeth and the Anglican communion.*

The church has been unhappy in its many divisions, there being today 23 denominations in America bearing the name "Methodist." In 1828 as a protest against episcopal authority, a group broke away to form the Methodist Protestant Church. In 1844 the church split north and south on the issue of slavery. Happily, these three branches were able to reunite in 1939 as The Methodist Church, its membership of 9,000,000 making it today the largest protestant denomination in America. There are in addition three large negro groups: The African Methodist Episcopal Church which organized in Philadelphia in 1787 and now has more than 1,100,000 members; the African Methodist Episcopal Zion Church which organized in New York in 1796 and has over 500,000 members; and the Colored Methodist Episcopal Church which was organized in the South in 1870 and has about 385,000 members. Combining all groups, the "Methodists" in America number substantially over 11,000,000 members.

The Methodist Church is a member of the World Methodist Conference, formerly known as the Methodist Ecumenical Council, which was established in 1870. This Conference, composed of delegates from 24 Methodist Churches, having their seats of government in 17 different countries, meets every five years and maintains a secretariat and office in London, for the eastern hemisphere, and in New York for the western hemisphere. Bishop Ivan Lee Holt serves as first President of the newly constituted World Methodist Conference.

The British Methodist Church does not have an episcopal form of government. Generally speaking those churches which came into being through English missionary effort have followed their form and those from American effort the episcopal form.

The World Methodist Conference has no legislative control over its constituent members. It meets on a fraternal basis and

---

* See paper "The Methodist Ministry" by Daniel L. Marsh.

makes plans for cooperative efforts in missionary work and world evangelism.

The Methodist Church has always been interested in the ecumenical movement and has taken an active part in the founding of the World Council of Churches in Amsterdam (1948) and the National Council of Churches in Cleveland (1950). A layman, Dr. John R. Mott, was one of the guiding spirits of the World Council and became its first Honorary President and Bishop Oxnam was elected to serve as one of the first Presidium.

The Protestant Episcopal Church (1789)

The Revolution that separated the colonies of the Atlantic seaboard from the English crown left the Anglican congregations isolated from the mother Church. The scattered parishes were completely disorganized and suffered acute financial distress. The civil establishments guaranteeing the support of the Church in the southern colonies were terminated by the new States; in the North the funds provided by the missionary body of the Church of England, the Society for the Propagation of the Gospel, were necessarily withdrawn. Moreover, the flight of a large number of Loyalists from the central and New England States to Canada and the West Indies removed from the Church many of its ablest clergy and lay leaders.

Between 1780 an 1783, the Rev. William White of Philadelphia and the Rev. William Smith of Maryland took steps to organize the clergy and laymen of the Middle States in the Protestant Episcopal Church, appealing to parishes elsewhere to join them. Meanwhile, the clergy of Connecticut, firmly convinced that no national organization should be completed until an American episcopate had been secured, sent the Rev. Samuel Seabury to England to seek consecration as bishop.

Though Seabury was courteously received, the existing ecclesiastical laws prevented the English bishops from consecrating a man who could not take the statutory oaths of allegiance to the King and supremacy of the state. As a result, Seabury went to Scotland. There, on November 14, 1784, he was consecrated by three bishops of the little independent Scottish Episcopal Church, a

14

body which had continued an heroic and precarious existence in Presbyterian Scotland ever since the revolution of 1688 had swept episcopacy out of the Church of Scotland.

The legal obstacles which prevented Seabury's consecration in England aroused the English archbishops to action. Within two years Parliament was persuaded to pass the enabling legislation that allowed William White and Samuel Provoost to be consecrated in Lambeth Palace Chapel in 1787 for the Dioceses of Pennsylvania and New York. In 1790 the American episcopate in the English line was completed by the consecration of James Madison.

The General Convention of 1789 saw the final achievement of national unity and organization in the Protestant Episcopal Church. Earlier conventions in 1785 and 1786, attacking the problems facing the Church, had laid the groundwork for their solution. In 1789 the adoption of the Prayer Book and the Constitution gave the American Church the formularies in which its doctrine, discipline and worship were enshrined. Anglicanism was no longer confined to Great Britain.*

The Episcopalians have been peculiarly free from splits; only The Reformed Episcopal Church, a relatively small group, broke away in 1873. The Church even survived the Civil War, when the other major denominations, the Baptists, Presbyterians and Methodists, divided. New England rectors became abolitionists and one southerner, Bishop Polk, became a general under Lee, but they remained in the same Church. The name of every absent southern bishop was called in the New York Convention of 1862; northern churchmen corresponded with southern throughout the war; Bishop McIlvane of Ohio and fighting Bishop Polk of Louisiana prayed for each other by name from their respective chancels every Sunday.

Today the Church numbers about 2,500,000 members.

The Protestant Episcopal Church is a member of the family of episcopal churches known as the Anglican Communion. All these churches, tracing their ancestry from the Church of England, recognize each others' ministries and interchange clergymen and

* From *Chapters in Church History* by P. M. Dawley.

15

communicants. Organizationally, each branch of the communion is independent but, because they are of one communion, there can never be any geographical overlapping of its bishops' jurisdictions.

The Lambeth Conference is a meeting held approximately every ten years of all bishops of the Anglican Communion under the presidency of the Archbishop of Canterbury. This conference has no legislative power but great influence throughout the communion. The Anglican Communion is estimated at 38,000,000 members living in all parts of the world.

The Episcopal Church has always been interested in the ecumenical movement. Its Bishop Brent in 1910 took the lead in founding what became the Faith and Order movement and, with others, in founding the Life and Work movement, the two movements which merged in 1948 to form the World Council of Churches. Presiding Bishop Sherrill was elected first President of the new National Council of Churches, organized in Cleveland in 1950.

The Membership of the Commissions

Each church has a commission of eighteen, six bishops, six other clergymen and six laymen, and these commissions are currently engaged in discussions. Their present memberships are:

THE PROTESTANT EPISCOPAL JOINT COMMISSION ON APPROACHES TO UNITY

BISHOPS:
HAROLD L. BOWEN
(resigned)
OLIVER J. HART
ROBERT F. GIBSON, JR.
(Vice-Chairman)
STEPHEN E. KEELER
(Chairman)
ARTHUR B. KINSOLVING II
HARWOOD STURTEVANT

OTHER CLERGYMEN:
CHARLES D. KEAN
(Secretary)
ALDEN D. KELLEY
GERALD G. MOORE
DONALD H. WATTLEY
THEODORE O. WEDEL
ALEXANDER C. ZABRISKIE

LAYMEN:
JOHN NICHOLAS BROWN
GORDON K. CHALMERS
HOWARD T. FOULKES
PAUL F. GOOD
JOHN C. SPAULDING
GEORGE F. THOMAS

THE METHODIST COMMISSION ON CHURCH UNION

BISHOPS:
LLOYD C. WICKE
W. T. WATKINS
IVAN LEE HOLT
(Chairman)
RICHARD C. RAINES
WILLIS J. KING

OTHER CLERGYMEN:
RUFUS C. BAKER
NOLAN B. HARMON
M. LAFAYETTE HARRIS
UMPHREY LEE
DANIEL L. MARSH
JOHN M. VERSTEEG

LAYMEN:
V. E. DANIEL
ROCKWELL F. CLANCY
DONALD ODELL
WALTER WINFIELD
PARKER
CHARLES C. PARLIN
(Secretary)
C. E. JORDAN

17

CHAPTER II

The Episcopal Church and Church Unity

By ALDEN DREW KELLEY

I

If anything has been learned in the last thirty years of ecumenical and "church unity" discussions, it is the futility of the consideration of "church unity" as an ideal or in the abstract. The unity
of the Christian Church to the degree that it has relevancy to the
present divisions of Christendom and is congruent with the experience of Christians must be explored within the context of
specific, concrete, and existent actualities. This is to say that it is
either hypocritical or self-deluding for a Lutheran, Congrega-
tionalist, Presbyterian, or Episcopalian to talk about "church
unity" in general. No such transcendental approach is possible to
finite men. And the failure to recognize our ideological presupposi-
tions and the conditioning circumstances of our socio-cultural environment leads inevitably to the absolutization of our fragmentary
and limited experiences. The only escape from this particular
form of idolatry is the honest admission of the relative and condi-
tional character of our respective viewpoints.

Accordingly, as an Episcopalian I am necessarily impelled to
begin any thinking about the problem of the unity of the churches
within the peculiar framework of the Episcopal Church and the
Anglican Communion. It would be my hope that such thought
would not be arrested in its development but might pass somewhat beyond its contextual particularities.

The exposition which follows makes no claim to originality;
its dependence on the thought of other members of this Commission, and on many not directly quoted, who have wrestled
valiantly with our common concern, is apparent. If this statement

has any merit it will be merely that of bringing a diversity of material together and into focus.

In its concern for "church unity" the Episcopal Church faces in two directions at once. To quote from a colleague on the faculty of my Seminary, "We dare not be content with contemplating any particular reintegrations. We cannot think and work in terms which would imply the exclusion of the great Roman Catholic Church or of the venerable churches of the East. Nor can we contemplate a unity which would ignore the various branches of Protestant Christendom." (P. V. Norwood, *Progress and Prospects in Christian Reunion.* Hale Memorial Sermon, 1929.)

The confusion resulting from this ambivalent attitude has surely been aggravated by the official statements of the Anglican Communion as a whole. On one hand there are the pronouncements of Lambeth and of the Episcopal Church in this country directed toward the Protestant world. On the other, there are such documents as the Reply of the Archbishops to Pope Leo XIII, the Lambeth statement to the Council of Rumanian Orthodox Church, and the Joint Statement of the Church of England and the Old Catholic Church at Bonn, which concordat has become the basis of intercommunion between the Polish National Catholic Church and the Protestant Episcopal Church in this country. I am not hinting that such more or less "official" formulae are political in intention and designed for external consumption depending on the group with which we are negotiating. They do represent multivarious aspects or emphases of the thought and life of the Episcopal Communion.

I should be less than frank if I did not point out that some groups within our church are happier with the thought of approaches to the churches of Episcopal order while other groups yearn most for strengthening of our bonds with the churches of Protestant tradition. Moreover, at times there have been situations where the right hand knew not what the left hand was doing, because the discussions and negotiations were carried on by separate committees or agencies. I think this situation is no longer so extreme; but it has served to befuddle the onlooker in the past.

19

The solution of these seemingly contradictory, or at least inconsistent, trends in unity approaches by the Episcopal Church is not to be found on the superficial level of ecclesiastical politics. It lies deep within the history of the Episcopal Church and the day by day experience of innumerable souls within its fold.

II

The Church as Community of Life

Perhaps we can get a hint of what is involved if we try to understand the unconscious drive for unity on a deeper level. Although the Episcopal Church has not been entirely indifferent to the "Life and Work" aspect of the Ecumenical Movement, it is obvious that its interest has not been as pronounced as the churches of American Protestantism nor even that of the Church of England. Its major concerns have been in the area of "Faith and Order."

The whole story lying back of this preference cannot be gone into here. However, it might be well to point out, in passing, that in large areas of this country, particularly the Middle West, the Episcopal Church is characterized by a *sect* life and mentality rather than the practice and thought usually associated with a *Church*. This is the case despite the fact that historically and theologically the Episcopal Church cannot be properly labeled as "sect." The invaluable distinction made by Ernest Troeltsch as between sect and church is carried over into much that is representative of the political, economic, and social viewpoint of Episcopal Churches as "sects." Withdrawal from the world, total condemnation of any hint of the secular, and lack of a sense of social or missionary responsibility are held almost as axiomatic by hundreds of parishes and missions of the Episcopal Church.

It should not be forgotten that the Episcopal Church has no monopoly on the sect attitude. As Charles Henry Brent said, even the Church of Rome finds itself in the United States as only one sect among many. All Christian bodies in this country exhibit a high degree of sectarianism; but in different areas. However, the Episcopal Church has on occasion been described as the most protesting sect in American Protestantism. In so far as this is true, it denies its avowedly churchly and Catholic character.

This one factor alone, although it is by no means the only one, would account for the lack of overwhelming interest of the Episcopal Church as a whole in the Life and Work movement.

To go on, neither has the concern of the Episcopal Church been equally for "Faith" and for "Order." It is generally recognized that if the problem of order can be settled, the problem of faith is not an insurmountable obstacle. In its dealings with churches of episcopal order the Episcopal Church both by itself and as a part of the Anglican Communion has made considerable progress. There will come to mind immediately certain Orthodox Churches of the East and the Old Catholics of western Europe and this country where there have been mutual recognition of "orders" resulting in intercommunion or permissive forms of limited intercommunion. Other examples are: (1) the relationship with the State Church of Sweden; (2) pre-war proposals for the conferring of the Episcopacy on the Church of Finland; (3) the cordial response of the House of Bishops of the Episcopal Church to the request for conferral of the Episcopacy on the Philippine National Church.

The rather wide variety of theological opinion held by the above-mentioned groups does not appear to Anglicans as a matter of final and supreme importance. Note one statement from the Bonn agreement, "Intercommunion does not require from either communion the acceptance of all doctrinal opinion, sacramental devotion, or liturgical practice characteristic of the other but implies that each believes the other to hold all the essentials of the Christian faith." The "essentials of the Christian faith," whatever they may be, are by no means ignored but one does get the feeling that intercommunion is ultimately more important than "unity" of faith if the latter means uniformity of belief.

Also, it is well known that time and time again even where the Episcopal Church has found a large measure of theological agreement with another Christian body, discussions have broken down whenever the problem of the ministry "rears its ugly head." Surely no one really thinks this is due to a neurotically obsessive idea of divine mission on the part of Episcopalians or a desire to put

21

over an obscurantist interpretation of the origin and nature of the Christian ministry, even though in the heat of debate Episcopalians may sound that way and their non-episcopal brethren have more than once suggested such was the case.

I suggest at least two factors which have reinforced this pre-occupation with Order by the Episcopal Church and which operate fairly continuously, usually on the unconscious level, in moulding the thought and practice of the Episcopal Church and its larger context, the Anglican Communion.

(1) The Episcopal Church and the Anglican Communion as a whole is *not* a "confessional" Church. This is rarely understood by those beyond the boundaries of Anglicanism and only occasionally within. The Thirty-Nine Articles of Religion, the Catechism, the Offices of Instruction, etc., have often been taken as "official confessions of faith." But both the Catechism and the Articles of Religion refer to the articles of *belief* or *faith* as the Apostles' and the Nicene Creed. Nothing could be more general, perhaps even vague, and to some people more unsatisfactory, than that.

We can see more clearly what is involved if we look at the recent statement on Faith and Order prepared by the Church's Joint Commission on Unity.

"The Apostles' Creed rehearses the mighty acts of God in creation, redemption, and sanctification as recorded in the Holy Scriptures. Upon these the life of the Church is based. As a declaration of allegiance to the Triune God the Apostles' Creed is a profession of faith appropriate to Holy Baptism."

"The Nicene Creed likewise witnesses to the faith of the historic Church in its assertion of fundamental Christian truth and its denial of fundamental errors, and is appropriate to Holy Communion."

"While liberty of interpretation may be allowed, the Christian faith as set forth in these two creeds ought to be received and believed by all Christian people."

It should be noted that both creeds are set within the framework of the cultic practice of the Church. Among other things one may conclude that the faith of the Episcopal Church is to be found implicitly in its worship rather than explicitly in an historic "confessional" document. Thus we are led to see that the Anglican fellowship is maintained or held together by factors other than "unity of faith." This is a matter of common understanding and experience among Episcopalians but a puzzle to many other Christian groups.

This means that in practice Episcopalians are first and foremost concerned with *community*. Community, as defined by Webster's *Unabridged Dictionary*, is "a body of people having *common* organizations or interests, or living in the same place and under the same laws and regulations." Community is different from "unity." There may be "community of life" without "unity of faith." On the other hand, "community" may be thought of as historically and psychologically prior to unity. If this seems to be another form of the "which comes first—the chicken or the egg" problem, then let us say that community and unity are mutually dependent. Theologically speaking, one might say that the relationship between community of life and unity of belief is a dialectical one; and historically speaking one could suggest that within the life of the Christian Church, community and unity are respectively the empirical forms of the notes of "Catholicity" and "Holiness."

The tendency of Anglicanism and the Episcopal Church, however, has been mainly in the direction of *community*, the unbroken fellowship, the Koinonia; accordingly, the emphasis on the ministry as the tie which binds the sacred community—temporally backwards to its origin as the People of God, the Old Israel—and spatially throughout the world. Hence, also, the centrality of its Liturgy as an expression of the common life of the Household of Faith.

(2) The second unconscious and determining factor in the peculiarly Anglican and Episcopalian approach may be arrived at in another way. This one is based on an obvious over-simplification of history but I trust, nevertheless, that the main point will meet with some degree of acceptance.

By and large the Church or Churches of the East have been from early Christian times preoccupied with orthodoxy. Heresy was and is the great sin. Not for nothing was the term "orthodox" popular in the East. Unity of belief must be maintained at any cost. Even schism is not too great a cost for that pearl beyond price.

Up to the time of the Protestant Reformation, the Church of the West, on the other hand, was supremely concerned with the community—the unity of the Body of Christ. Not for nothing was the term "Catholic" preferred. Great divergence of opinion was tolerated unless it seemed to be disruptive of the common life. Schism was the great sin. Peace within the body was willingly paid for even at the price of almost constant theological controversy.

Now, as has been pointed out by Troeltsch, the conflict between Roman Catholic and Continental Reformation doctrinal views was not so much "doctrinal" as an "opposition to Catholic practice (Praxis)." The reformed bodies took over uncritically much of the late medieval popular theology, sometimes of the worst sort, and their own special doctrinal viewpoints were developed, at least in part, as a bulwark against the rejected cultic practices of the medieval western Church.

Assuredly the "reformation" of the Church of England was singularly untheological. There is no such thing as "Cranmerism" in the doctrinal tradition of the Anglican Communion; in fact there is not even such a word. On the theological front, to quote Theodore O. Wedel (*Journal of Religious Thought,* Vol. IV, No. 1), "it tagged along behind the more voluble continental reformation revolt and, when pressed, accepted the major theological achievements of the Reformers. Evangelical fervor has certainly not been absent from its life. But 'Common Prayer' has always come first." The results of Protestant Reformation thinking were assimilated within Catholic Order; and where that seemed impossible they were ignored.

The Counter-Reformation came to believe that heresy inevitably led to schism, reversed the traditional view of the West and attempted to impose a complete and uniform doctrinal system on the Churches of Roman obedience.

The Church of England, and later the Anglican Communion as a whole, was but little touched by the shift from the community of

24

worship and work to unity of belief and stands today as about the only inheritor of the western tradition.

Apart from any value judgments we may be tempted to make, I think the foregoing analysis does clarify three things about the unity concerns of the Episcopalian Church. First, the deep intellectual conviction and high enthusiasm which the *idea* of unity or community has for Episcopalians. Secondly, the failure in fact to realize much progress in unity approaches with non-episcopal Protestant Christianity. Thirdly, the insistence, obstinacy—if you wish—with which we turn again and again to the question of the Ministry, which is ultimately to say, the Community, the Body of Christ, the Church which includes, in the words of the Faith and Order statement of the Unity Commission, "The principles of a distinctive ministry, as an original element but not the sole constitutive element in the life of the Church," and regards the historic Episcopate, in the language of Cyprian, as the "glue" of the Church.

Community characterized by mutual dependence of its members one with another and its individual members with the whole, by fellowship, and by a common purpose is deeply yearned for as an expression of fundamental human solidarity. But "with men it is impossible." However, many would agree with V. A. Demant's statement in *Union of Christendom* (edited by the Bishop of Brechin). "The Church is the only true community on earth because its bond of union is not human, and the common life it shares, the common purposes of its members, are not their own; they are given from beyond. In the Church men are one body, not because they like one another, nor because they happen to agree upon this or that truth."

"Members of the Body of Christ know that all true solidarity springs out of the strength, not the weakness, of the parties. The modern world starts from the autonomous individual and tries to make him a social being, or from the disintegrated state and tries to make it an international co-operator. But it cannot be done. Men and nations cannot enter into true social relationship because man is empty and the state is the lackey of its many lords. All the creaking effort to be brotherly, social and international is

25

the external attempt to make up for an internal defect, a defect of unity with the whole of reality. . . . If he (man) is to be a good neighbor he must be a true person; he is a true person only by his relation to God and his activities in God. . . . the second commandment of the Gospel rests upon the first."

We should now consider the opposite term of the basic polarity between *community* of life and *unity* of faith. It would be quite a false impression if we were left with the view that community, even though regarded as the necessary organic structure within which the processes of truth are developed and expressed, is sufficient unto itself. An exclusive emphasis on community and order results in only a partial, and sometimes merely a partisan, presentation of the existential possibilities of a renewed and reunited Christendom. The dialectical, or if it is preferred—the polar, principle of unity must be held together with the principle of community, to do justice to full-orbed Christianity.

III

Unity in Truth

For a moment we should stop and take a look at the common phrase "unity in truth." In terms of modern studies in semantics it is an impossible one; it consists of two highly abstract words related by an ambiguous preposition. What we are trying to say is more precisely expressed, I think, by the phrase "agreement(s) in (the area of) belief(s)." * That some such minimum agreement is necessary seems to be implied by the Bonn statement, "Intercommunion does not require from either communion the acceptance of doctrinal opinion . . . characteristic of the other but implies that each believes the other to hold all the *essentials of the Christian faith*." (Italics mine.)

Moreover, in the *Chicago Quadrilateral* (1886) we read, "We do hereby affirm that the Christian unity now so earnestly desired can be restored only by the return of all Christian communions to

---

* This is still far removed from the realm of concrete reality even though it is a step nearer than "unity in truth." A still better statement would be, "The Beliefs of man1, man2, man3, etc., are near enough to each to permit some degree of common response to the same object, and common action." But this is too awkward for ordinary literary usage.

the principles of unity exemplified by the undivided Catholic Church during the first ages of its existence; which principles we believe to be *the substantial deposit of Christian Faith* and Order committed by Christ and His Apostles to the Church unto the end of the world. (Again, italics are mine.) . . . As inherent parts of this sacred deposit, and therefore as essential to the restoration of unity among the divided branches of Christendom, we account the following": And there follow the four points, so-called, of the *Quadrilateral;* the first two dealing with the faith of the church, the third with its cultic practice, and the fourth with its order.

In the words of the Lambeth Council (1888) these first two points are: (1) "The Holy Scriptures of the Old and New Testament as 'containing all things necessary to salvation' and as being the rule and ultimate standard of faith." (For the noninclusion of the Apocrypha see Articles of Religion VI.)

(2) "The Apostles' Creed as the Baptismal symbol; the Nicene Creed as the sufficient statement of the Christian faith."

The foregoing quotations are enough to illustrate the meaning and implications, perhaps at times unconscious, of what we mean in the Episcopal Church by "agreement in belief." These are: (1) A necessary minimum of common belief as both a means to true and basic unity, or community, and as an expression of same. (2) This common belief is set forth and held within a common context, or social framework, i.e. the Church. (3) The norm or ultimate standard is found by appeal to Scripture and Tradition. (4) Over, above, and along with the minimum "essentials of the Christian Faith" there are diverse beliefs permissible and valuable. In a more generalized way we can say, *"In necessariis unitas; in dubiis libertas";* and changing the usual meaning from "in all things" to "among all" (members of the Body), *"in omnibus caritas."*

Let us now discuss briefly these four implications in order. First, it is commonly accepted that some sort of doctrinal agreement is a means of arriving at the reunion of Christendom. This presupposition lies back of the Faith and Order Conferences, the South India Church scheme, the discussions of the Episcopal Church with various religious bodies in this country, such documents— *The Concordat, Joint Ordination, Basic Principles,* and *The Pro-*

27

posed Basis of Union—as resulted from negotiations with the Presbyterian Church in the United States of America, and the high tension debates within our own Communion. The assumption that agreement of belief is the necessary means to union is often an unconscious, unanalyzed and uncriticized one. There is no evidence in history that formal and verbal agreements have ever effectively brought together human institutions. Institutions have been "merged" by the superior power of one over the other, by a common purpose, or by a common life. No one who appreciates the significance of the modern theory of the sociological basis of thought and knowledge could possibly subscribe to the view that having achieved some sort of *verbal* agreement unity would follow automatically.

Along the same line, it is generally forgotten, or ignored, that more often than not agreement in belief is an *expression* of a common life rather than being the basis of it. This point need not be labored because the reader will be familiar with the contributions of students of the history of religions, of modern sociologists, of Marx, and of Freud, whose insights cannot be ignored even though we may not find acceptable all or even more than a small part of their conclusions.

Secondly, and this follows in part from the previous paragraph, a common faith or belief is only properly understood in its full significance within the group wherein it is held. Verbalizations of opinions out of context, *in vacuo,* are meaningless. Words mean what they mean only within a certain framework of reference, and the frame is supplied by the group within which the utterances take place. Many examples will come readily to mind but let us take one or two which have immediate bearing on our discussion.

When a Roman Catholic says "Jesus is God," he means one thing by that statement; when a modern religious humanist says, "Jesus is God," it sounds identical with, or at least similar to, the former utterance. Of course, the meanings are about as contradictory as can be found. (Just in passing, to me both statements are not only wrong but absurd.)

Again, the "points" of the *Lambeth Quadrilateral*—what do they mean? Whatever their meaning is, it can be found only within

28

the life and thought of the Anglican Communion. The bizarre view that they have a meaning in and of themselves has led to the all too-common interpretation that they represent points of discussion with any and all ecclesiastical bodies who may be interested in the possibility of reunion; that is, for example, we say what we think is meant by the "historic episcopate"; then the "Unionites" say what they think; and ultimately we shall arrive at some higher synthesis or lower compromise of interpretation quite different from the view of the Ministry held explicitly or implicitly within the Episcopal Church. And this fantastic result is called assent to the *Quadrilateral!* A common view of the ministry can be achieved, if at all, only by a common experience within the one community.

"If ye abide in my word then are ye truly my disciples; and ye shall know the truth, and the truth shall make you free." Commenting on these words from the fourth Gospel, the Rt. Rev. Eric Graham, the late Bishop of Exeter, wrote, "First the venture of faith; then the discipleship; then knowledge of the truth; and with that knowledge, liberty; this seems to be the order of the stages in the Christian life as our Lord here gives them. . . . But it is to be noted that it is not liberty which is the way to truth, but truth which is the way to liberty." And we might also note that discipleship, life within the covenanted community, precedes the knowing of the truth.

Is not this thought echoed in the opening sermon to the Edinburgh Conference in 1937, delivered by William Temple? "Our faith must be more than the trust which leads us to rely upon (Christ): it must be the deeper faith which leads us to wait for him. It is not we who can heal the wounds in his Body. We confer and deliberate, and that is right. But it is not by contrivance and adjustment that we can unite the Church of God. It is only by coming closer to him that we can draw nearer to one another. . . . Only when God has drawn us closer to himself shall we be truly united together; and then our task will be, not to consummate our endeavor but to register his achievement."

Thirdly, the norm or ultimate standard is found by appeal to Scripture and tradition. Note that this is not an appeal to

Scripture *and* an appeal to tradition. In a sense the two are one because Scripture, both the Old Testament and the writings which became known as the New Testament, were part of the tradition of the early Church. Modern Biblical studies have shown that, for example, the portrait of Christ set forth in the New Testament came out of the early tradition which was expressed in part by the books later accepted as canonical. It was by the tradition, which was regarded as the Apostolic teaching, that the manifold literature of the early Church was judged and certain writings selected as being most in accord with the faith of the Church. Moreover, the interpretation of Scripture has been based for the most part, within the main stream of Christian life and thought, on the insights of the Fathers and the continuing and developing understanding of innumerable others within the covenant community. But it is as expositors of Scripture and not as originators or maintainers of some tradition apart from Scripture they have been accepted.

Although the Scriptures may be thought of as "the rule and standard of faith" and as "containing all things necessary to salvation" and the Nicene Creed may be received as "the sufficient statement of the Christian Faith" the agreement on faith and practice of the Church has gone beyond these in actuality. The Scriptures and the Creed cannot be regarded as a manual of public worship, ecclesiastical discipline, and other necessary elements in the life of the Church; these things belong to the sphere of tradition. In a letter, dated 1552, to the Privy Council, Cranmer wrote, "They say that kneeling (to receive Holy Communion) is not commanded in the Scripture: and that what is not commanded in Scripture is unlawful. There is the root error of the sects! If that be true, take away the whole Service Book and let us have no more trouble in setting forth an order in religion, or indeed in common policy. If kneeling be not expressly enjoined in Holy Scripture, neither is standing or sitting. Let them lie down on the ground and eat their meals like Turks or Tartars."

None of the foregoing is to deny that having once recognized and accepted it, Scripture acquires an ultimacy and a unique autonomy of its own. The Faith and Order statement issued in

30

1948 by the Joint Commission on Unity of the Episcopal Church reads as follows: "The Holy Scriptures are the inspired record of God's self-revelation to man and of man's response to that revelation. This is the primary ground of the authority of the Scriptures. The fact that the Church under the guidance of the Holy Spirit has accepted the Bible as canonical invests it as a whole with an authoritative character for all Christians. Its authority is further validated by the continuing experience of Christian people. . . . The Bible has been and is for the Christian Church the ultimate criterion of its teaching and the chief source of guidance for its life. It contains all doctrine required for salvation through faith in Jesus Christ."

In short, Tradition is in great part dependent on the Scriptures *and* the Scriptures, their authority, and interpretation are in great part dependent on Tradition.

Fourthly, over, above, and along with "the essentials of the Christian Faith" are many permissable, valuable and diverse beliefs. Much of what might be said here has been covered, at least by implication, in the preceding discussion of Scripture and tradition. However, we must realize that diversity of belief does present a rather terrifying picture to many people. I use the word "terrifying" advisedly because the rejection of diversity of faith for a uniform and monolithic theological structure is due, in my opinion, to emotional causes rather than intellectual obstacles. The seductiveness of the completely simple, non-contradictory, and "logical" (meaning in accordance with Aristotelian logic) *system* must, like "the power of a woman, never be underestimated." Many are the criticisms of the "system" or "systems" in our day, but the emotionally insecure who are striving for external and authoritative assurance *cannot* but treat such criticism as a personal attack and thus instinctively reject it.

Nevertheless the Church recognizes and has recognized in varying ways that although there is an "essential faith" there is also an accompanying diversity of faiths or beliefs. At times it has been willing to tolerate such and in other periods, usually when the Church was weaker, it has tried to suppress deviations from

31

the party line. This ebb and flow has a noticeable parallel in the kingdoms of the world.

What seems to me important to realize is that *diversity* of belief is as much a part of the life of the Church as *unity* of belief. As there is one Spirit but a diversity of gifts, so there is but one Revelation but a diversity of experience and responses. Note that this is not merely a diversity of understanding or response but of "objective experiences" or events. There has been always a great temptation to avoid the full impact of the existence of diversities by retreating to some formula which denies the richly diverse complex of reality, by saying in effect that man's intellectual and emotional responses are varied but the reality which encompasses him is a smooth, uniform, and rational *it*.

Life in the family, as a type family, does not require an absolute point to point correlation of belief among the members of the family. In fact, even if such were possible nothing more hideous could be imagined. In fact the family would be dead, because it is only on the level of inorganic matter that everything becomes close to an abstract measurable uniformity. It is out of the creative inter-play of diverse personalities that family life is even tolerable, to say nothing of the possibility of growth and realization of its rich potentialities.

IV

Community and Unity

As life and thought cannot be separated except by an arbitrary and artificial act of the intellect, so, too, community of life and unity of belief. The two must be held together in thought as they are in reality. This may mean some tension, because there are at times seemingly irresoluble elements in the relationship between community of life and unity of thought; something of the same sort as is found in the relation between authority and freedom, the group and the individual, the Trinity in the Unity, and so on.

One approach to the polar relationship between "community" and "unity" might be suggested. A recent popular book of Nels

32

Ferre sets forth the Scriptures, reason, personal religious experience, the church, etc., as "pillars of faith." We could turn these around and regard them from the "divine super-perspective," to use a phrase from another book of Ferre, and see in them varied means whereby the Revelation of God comes to man. To assert that God's sovereign will and purpose is revealed only through reason or the Scriptures or the Church or what have you would be false—a distortion and a limitation of the power of God. "At sundry times and in divers manners," God has spoken and speaks to men.

Following this line of thought, God's purpose may be worked out *both* through "His People" and the Word which He speaks to them through Scripture and Tradition; but neither may be thought of as the exclusive, nor even the primary, instrument of His revelation and redemption.

Isn't it just at this point where we find the great watershed in Christendom? Are not the divisions in Christianity due in part to the absolutization of the Church on one hand and the absolutization of the Scriptural Word on the other? Both forms of Christianity forget that back of the Church and back of the Scriptures lies the only Absolute, God himself. Both forget the intrinsic relativity of all created things.

The unity of faith, derived from Scripture and Tradition, and the community of life, in which unity of faith is born and grows and which is at the same time dependent on agreement in belief for its full realization—these two are inextricably, irrevocably, and mutually interdependent. Within the life and thought of the Episcopal Church this hard fact has been only partially realized— actually it is often denied. It may be the purpose of God that our vocation will be increasingly understood by ourselves and accordingly it may become more and more evident to others that the *koinonia tou pneumatou hagiou* cannot be attained at the expense of the *logos tou theou,* nor the Word of God maintained by the sacrifice of the Holy Fellowship.

"And they continued stedfastly in the apostles' doctrine *and* fellowship . . . (Acts 2 :42*a*).

V

Intercommunion

It has been generally assumed in the Episcopal Church that intercommunion should be the expression of the consummation of union rather than a means for the achievement of unity. Resolution 42 of the Lambeth Conference of 1930 reads: "The Conference, maintaining as a general principle that intercommunion should be the goal of, rather than a means to, the restoration of union. . . ." If the foregoing discussion of the need for restoration of the Fellowship of the Holy Spirit has any merit then the question must be raised again as to the validity of the above common assumption. *

Immediately it should be understood that the discussion which follows is not intended to have any direct bearing on the "open communion" controversy. Furthermore, for the purpose of orderly consideration the problem of the Ministry will have to be postponed.

To proceed: it seems quite clear that in the early centuries, and later, the gift made available through Communion was in order that "all may be one." This theme is repeated in the ancient liturgies and finds explicit expression in the writings of Augustine. "This is the sacrifice of Christians, 'the many one Body in Christ' which thing the Church celebrates in the sacrament of the altar, wherein it is shown her that in this thing which she offers she herself is offered to God." (*de Civitate Dei*.) In fact it is the Body of Christ as the Church which is on the altar and which is offered to God. In Thomas Aquinas the special eucharistic gift is unity with our Lord and with each other. "The spiritual benefit received in the Sacrament is the unity of the mystical Body." (*Summa Theologiae,* P. 3, Q.73, A.3.)

The Church is held together and united in its common cult practice. Not only did it continue in the apostles doctrine and fellowship but also "in the breaking of bread, and in the prayers." But today it is in its differences in worship that the greatest divisive-

---

* See Lambeth 1948 for reaffirmation of foregoing view in criticism of the "Cambridge Sermon" (1946) of the Archbishop of Canterbury.

ness in Christianity is found. T. A. Lacey in an almost Chestertonian paradox wrote: "It is theology which unites us and religion which divides us."

It is becoming increasingly apparent to all Christians that, along with the problem of the ministry, the problem of liturgical practice is as central. From the viewpoint of the Episcopal Church the two issues are in a sense one. Here I would quote the wise words of Theodore O. Wedel: "Whenever Anglicanism is brought into ecumenical debate, attention usually becomes focused upon its polity and specifically upon its episcopacy. This is, I think, unfortunate. The problems connected with Anglican Church order ought really to be secondary. The episcopate, as it is cherished in Anglican Church life, can never be fully understood unless it is seen as guardian of something more fundamental—the cult. The Bishop, in Anglican feeling (if not in its rationalized apologetic), is first of all a cultic and sacramental figure. He is the 'great' minister of the 'great church,' a church unified by a common liturgical loyalty, common symbols, common prayers, a common eucharist."

The Episcopal Church is differentiated from all other "Reformation communions" most of all by its liturgy, etc. It is a Church in which "cult and liturgy are placed at the very center of church life, emphasized in importance as in no other 'reformed' church body. Loyalty to the Prayer Book replaces subscription to a confession or the warm fellowship life of the sect." (T. O. Wedel.)

The Way of Worship by Scott Francis Brenner, a minister of the Evangelical and Reformed Church body, is an effort to set forth an "ecumenical liturgy" as the basis of church reunion.

All this is to illustrate that we are coming to appreciate that the liturgy is actually *creative* of the Fellowship and not only expressive of it. It does not seem that this is fully understood by members of the Episcopal Church, although its unconscious apprehension may account for the retention of the eucharist as central in the life of the Episcopal Church.

At the 1946 General Convention in Philadelphia, the empowering resolution for the continuation of the Joint Commission on Approaches to Unity reads in part as follows: "and (the Commission) be requested to prepare a statement of faith and order, in harmony with the *Lambeth Quadrilateral,* upon which the Protestant Episcopal Church in the U.S.A. is prepared to enter into intercommunion and to proceed toward organic federation with the Presbyterian Church in the U.S.A., or with any other interested Christian body . . ." It would be bold to assert that this was a carefully thought out plan comprehending the stages through which the Episcopal Church must pass before realizing "organic union" as proposed at General Convention (1937) in the *Declaration of Purpose.* However, we might see in this, possibly inadvertent, order of steps which seem to indicate that intercommunion should come first, further evidence of the developing apprehension of the priority and creative power of the common liturgy for the Fellowship.

If some way could be devised for the inclusion within our liturgical life of those baptized Christians who are "outside" of the ordinary discipline of the Episcopal Church, then, indubitably, one of the greatest steps forward in the restoration of the Christian Community would have been taken. A like starting place might be found by going back to the principles of the 1919 *Proposals for an Approach Toward Unity by a Conference of Episcopalians and Congregationalists.* This was an unofficial statement signed by a number of eminent and representative clergymen of the Episcopal Church including: Hughell Fosbroke, William Manning, Philip M. Rhinelander, Edmund Rousmaniere, Charles Slattery, Howard B. St. George, George Craig Stewart, and Boyd Vincent.

I quote from the *Proposals:* "We are agreed that it is our Lord's purpose that believers in Him should be one visible society. Into such a society, which we recognize as the Holy Catholic Church, they are initiated by Baptism; whereby they are admitted to fellowship with one another. The unity which is essential to his Church's effective witness and work in the world must express and maintain this fellowship. It cannot be fully realized without community of worship, faith and order, including common participation in the Lord's Supper."

"To give full effect to those principles in relation to the churches to which we respectively belong requires some form of corporate

36

union . . . In this situation *we believe that a practical approach toward eventual union may be made by the establishment of intercommunion in particular instances."* (Italics mine.)

The *Proposals* go on to suggest a "form of canonical sanction" whereby the ministers of other communions may, without giving up their ministry in the communion to which they belong, be episcopally ordained. This suggestion eventuated in Canon 36, *Of the Ordination of Deacons and Priests in Special Cases.* Many are persuaded that the present canon, and the Ordination formula embodied therein, is unsatisfactory, if not defective and unconstitutional. Be that as it may, we can conclude that what was really unsatisfactory and "defective" was the action, or lack of it, and the attitudes of the general church for the past thirty years, which have prevented the following through of the wisdom of better men than we in our generation.

Eventually, such an arrangement would have to be reciprocal for it to be genuine *intercommunion;* and there is the crux of the problem for the Episcopal Church. *"Intercommunion* between two churches is understood as meaning that members of either church shall be permitted to receive the Holy Communion in the other and that ministers of either church shall be competent to celebrate the Holy Communion in the other." (Statement on Faith and Order. 1948. Unity Commission.) (As a matter of interest we might note that this definition goes beyond the basis of intercommunion as set forth in the Bonn agreement, which makes no reference to "ministers" and their competence "to celebrate the Holy Communion in the other."

To the solution of the problem of intercommunion we are called *today*—to give our deep attention and most serious thought. It cannot be by-passed, and it deserves the study of the best minds of the Episcopal Church.

As has been pointed out heretofore, no matter where our thinking begins we end up facing the same issue, the problem of Order or the Ministry. For the Episcopal Church the possibilities of intercommunion includes inevitably the *fact* and the *theory* of the ministry. The two questions are one and must be worked through together.

VI

Church Order

Any detailed explication of the problem of Church Order would not seem to be required within the terms of our immediate concern. Its centrality has been indicated. But agreement must first be achieved as to whether it shall be discussed within the context of mere constitutional arrangement or in terms of its functional character in the Christian Community. Is the Ministry related only externally and mechanically to the ongoing historic fellowship or are its relations internal and organic? That question must be given priority over all other considerations. This seems to me to be the burden of so much that Charles Clayton Morrison asserts in his notable *What Is Christianity?*

The beginning of an answer to these problems is implied in the famous University of Cambridge sermon by the present Archbishop of Canterbury. I take the liberty of quoting from the Sermon words which are undoubtedly familiar to all: "As I have suggested the road is not yet open, we are not yet ready for organic or constitutional union. But there can be a process of assimilation, of growing alike. What we need is that while the folds remain distinct, there should be a movement towards a free and unfettered exchange of life in worship and sacrament between them as there is already of prayer and thought and Christian fellowship—in short that they should grow towards that full communion with one another, which already in their separation they have with Christ."

To continue, "At the Lausanne Conference of Churches in 1927, it was said that in view of the place which the episcopate, the Council of Presbyters, and the Congregation of the Faithful respectively had in the constitution of the early Church, in view of the fact that these three elements are each today and have been for centuries accepted by great Communions in Christendom, and that they are believed by many to be essential to the good order of the Church, 'We recognize that these several elements must all . . . have an appropriate place in the order of life of a reunited Church.' Every constitutional scheme has proceeded on those lines. The non-Episcopal churches have accepted the principle that episco-

38

pacy must exist along with the other elements in a reunited Church. For reasons obvious enough in Church History, they fear what may be made of episcopacy. But they accept the fact of it. If they do so for a reunited Church, why not also and earlier for the process of assimilation, as a step toward full communion? It may be said that in a reunited Church they could guard themselves in the constitution against abuses of episcopacy. But they could do so far more effectively by taking it into their own system. The Church of England has not yet found the finally satisfying use of episcopacy in practice; nor certainly has the Church of Rome. If non-Episcopal Churches agree that it must come into the picture, could they not take it and try it out on heir own ground first?"

"It is not of course quite as simple as all that. There are requirements and functions which Catholic tradition attaches to the office of a Bishop in the Church of God, which, if our aim is assimilation and full communion, must be safeguarded. Negotiators in the past have been able to agree upon them, and could with hope enquire into them further, if our non-episcopal brethren were able to contemplate the step I suggest. As it seems to me, it is an easier step for them to contemplate than those involved in a union of churches: and if achieved, it would immensely carry us forward toward full communion, without the fearful complexities and upheavals of a constitutional union."

The Archbishop goes on, "It is because I fear a stalemate, that I venture to put this suggestion forward for examination. I love the Church of England, as the Presbyterian and the Methodist love their churches. It is, I think, not possible yet nor desirable that any church should merge its identity in a newly constituted union. What I desire is that I should be able freely to enter their churches and they mine in the Sacraments of the Lord and in the full fellowship of worship, that His life may freely circulate between us. Cannot we grow to full communion with each other before we start to write a constitution? If there were agreement on it, I would thankfully receive at the hands of others their commission in their accustomed form and in the same way confer our own; that is the mutual exchange of love and enrichment to which Lambeth, 1920, called us."

That this proposal is not without its difficulties is apparent to all; and they have been underlined by the report of the conversations between representatives of the Archbishop of Canterbury and representatives of the Evangelical Free Churches in England.* Nevertheless, and with full cognizance of the seemingly insurmountable obstacles, it is my present opinion that through some such device making possible intercommunion the most likely avenue to church union will be opened.

VII

Conclusion

By way of conclusion there are one or two things to be said.

The approaches to church unity made by the Episcopal Church and by other religious bodies have been, and still are, in most instances self-frustrating; they are not radical enough. There has not been on our part truly humble, rigorous, and deep thinking about the Church and its significance as the Community before God. We have not had the courage to seek, with God's help, guidance from the early Christian Fellowship, biblical, apostolical, and ecumenical. Our tendency has been to think and work for the unity of the Church by trying to synthesize the broken fragments of postmedieval Western Christianity. This criticism can be made of every church unity scheme in recent years. We should take counsel from the words of the *Chicago Quadrilateral:* "We do hereby affirm that the Christian unity now so earnestly sought can be restored only by the return of all Christian communions to the *principles* of unity exemplified by the undivided Catholic Church during the first ages of its existence." (Italics mine.)

Moreover, our efforts have been, mainly, reunion by formula. The futility of such an approach has been sufficiently discussed in an earlier part of this essay. This point was clearly indicated by Charles Henry Brent in his assertion that "the way to unity is to practice fellowship." To use the jargon of our day, unity must begin and be worked out on "the level" of local churches; it will not be achieved by discussion on "the top policy-making level."

---

* *Church Relations in England.* S.P.C.K. 1950.

In fact, the establishment of commissions, committees, and so on to do the unity work for the Church is sometimes for the local parish, the individual minister, or layman a means of escape from the dreadful burden put on all of us that God's Will may be done. We have appointed a committee and given it an expense account; it is the committee's job to find a way to unity—that is what it is paid for. Why should we worry? This implies the discredited psychology of the professional army for the state or the "professional" clergy for the Church. It is an evasion of personal responsibility as much as expecting the public schools to educate our children and the police force to preserve our morals. It does not work even in the case of the United Nations. It just won't do!

Through "practice of fellowship"—living with each other, praying with each other, thinking with each other—under the sovereign power of God, then will come unity and then only. And the victory will be His and His alone.

41

CHAPTER III

World Implications of Organic Union

By NOLAN B. HARMON

I have been asked to prepare a paper upon the subject of "The relationship of the Churches (now discussing a possible union) with their own world fellowships in the event of such a union." As is explained in a paper which I shall presently read, and which is part of this report, the respective Churches here represented are each very anxious to keep and hold all ties which now bind them to their respective world-wide fellowships. Specifically, the question arises: "What would be the attitude of the Church of England to any merger with The Methodist Church which the Protestant Episcopal might consummate; and what would world-wide Methodism have to say about the union of The Methodist Church of America with the Protestant Episcopal Church?

Answering the latter question first, I am quite certain there would be no appreciable effect in any formal or tangible way. On the contrary, I am quite certain that there would be a feeling of happy approval on the part of the Methodists the world over should their American brethren announce that they had entered into and created a larger fellowship, and had become a part of a larger Church. The Church of Canada may be used as an illustration here. In that Church the Methodist Church of Canada merged its life some time ago, but rather than losing our Canadian Methodist brethren, we have found through them a larger fellowship. The Church of Canada sends a fraternal delegate to our Methodist General Conference each four years, and in turn American Methodism sends a fraternal delegate to represent it before the "official gathering" of the Church of Canada.

As to what might be the attitude of the Lambeth Conference of the Church of England, to our proposed merger it is not possible of course to say at the present time. The Church of England has not yet extended full recognition to the Church of South India (which represents a union of different denominations) though it is understood that there are certain unusual situations in case of the South Indian Church which are holding the matter in abeyance. Naturally, the Protestant Episcopal Church will wish to consider very carefully whether any action it might take for a larger unity in this land might break some very precious ties which it has with the great Communion of which it has long been a part.

Now in dealing with Methodism, or the Methodist connection, I feel much more sure of my ground. Methodism has sometimes been called a *movement* rather than a Church. To be sure, it crystallizes into "churches" in different lands, but these are not all alike. Some are Episcopal Churches, having Bishops after the unusual pattern of Episcopacy which we have developed in American Methodism; some Methodists do not hold to episcopacy of any sort—as for instance the Church of Canada and The Methodist Church of England. These churches may be called "conciliar churches," as their respective conferences are authoritative, and the final sovereignty rests with the conference itself. However, no Methodist would ever stickle over the particular form of organization which his brother Methodists decide to follow in any particular date or region. We do have an ecumenical or world-wide conference, the next session of which will meet this coming Summer.* In this the Methodist Churches and groups over the world meet and there they send their representatives to exchange ideas and to speak regarding their common cause. But nothing that this conference does can be considered binding upon the individual Methodist bodies, and it is a sort of hands-across-the-seas fellowship only. So if it should come about that American Methodism should decide to unite with any church or churches here, all Methodists would feel that such a move would be no concern of other Methodists in other places. They would simply wish for us, as we should wish for ourselves, every success and happiness in the wider relationship.

Certain of the questions which I have discussed in the para-

---

* This was written early in 1951.

graphs above are further explained in a paper which I am attaching to this paper. The paper, which I mark "A" and hereby make a part of this report, was written by Bishop Ivan Lee Holt and will express better than I have done certain other aspects of this general problem.

Now may I venture to discuss, on a somewhat broader basis, certain of the problems which divide us? It may be also that certain of the information which I shall give will be informative and helpful to you brethren of the Protestant Episcopal Church.

As to doctrine, I do not believe there would be any great difference between the Methodist and Episcopal bodies. The twenty-five Articles of Religion which we have in our *Book of Discipline* were taken from the thirty-nine Articles of the Church of England. This was done by John Wesley himself who abridged the thirty-nine Articles and sent this abridgment on the Articles in a similar abridgment of the *Book of Common Prayer*. Naturally, Methodists are not likely to admit that he left out anything which an evangelical Christian may feel is of the essence of the faith. One article, that affirming the descent into hell, he did strike out from among the Articles, but he kept in the *text* of the Apostles' Creed (which he sent to American Methodism only in the Office for Adult Baptism) an affirmation "he descended into hell." I may say that the American Methodists almost at once took that out of the Creed—in 1786.

The liturgy which Mr. John Wesley sent to American Methodism was, as said above, an abridgment of the *Book of Common Prayer* of the Church of England. He stated in his preface to his edition of the Prayer Book "I believe that there is no liturgy either in ancient or modern times, which breathes more of scriptural, rational piety than the Common Prayer of the Church of England. And though the main of it was composed more than 200 years ago, yet is the language of it both strong and elegant. Little alteration is made in the following edition of it."

This book, which Mr. Wesley called "The Sunday Service for the Methodists in North America" was brought over to this country and was taken by the organizing Methodist Conference as its official norm of life and work. The ministers who

44

were ordained by the organizing conference of the Methodist Episcopal Church were ordained "according to the forms annexed to the liturgy of the Rev. John Wesley." These forms were an exact replica of the Ordinal of the Church of England, except that Mr. Wesley changed the word *priest* to *elder,* and *bishop* to *superintendent.* To this day Methodism continues to ordain her men exactly in accordance with these forms, except that we have put the word *bishop* in place of the word *superintendent* although we do keep the word *elder* for our second, or highest order, in the Methodist Church.

American Methodism, however, was not destined to become a liturgical church. The "Sunday Service" was discarded after a few years, though the Communion Service and the occasional offices in the back of the liturgy were retained and are published today in our Methodist *Book of Discipline* under the title "The Ritual." This accounts for the fact that our marriage service, our burial service, our Communion and forms for Ordination are so amazingly like those of the Protestant Episcopal Church. In fact, our Communion Service, which has hardly been changed at all, is that of the Church of England rather than that of the Protestant Episcopal Church in this country.

Now when it comes to polity, American Methodism is a highly centralized organization. Our Bishops, while not a third order ecclesiastically, do represent tremendous power as church executives. In our theory, the Bishop is an elder "set apart" for a particular kind of work. By virtue of the development which our church has undergone in American life, the Methodist bishop, because of his right and duty to "station the preachers," has gathered unto himself tremendous power. That power is modified and held in check of course by the General Conference and by the Constitution of the Methodist Church. But it is a very real power, and the Methodist Church is in essence, if not in name, an Episcopal Church in the full administrative sense of that term.

By holding on to the Article of Religion which states that the rites and ceremonies of churches need not always be the same, the Methodist Church makes allowances for other denominations—their rites, their ceremonies, their customs, their manners. We

45

have never been narrow in our *polity* nor in our *doctrine*. If we have been narrow at all, it has been in our *discipline,* and there is the situation which is frankly to be faced.

Methodist discipline, or the rules of life which the Methodist people have adopted for their personal conduct, has indeed been strict. It has been called narrow, and perhaps it was in the early days. But every Methodist the world over is expected to adhere to the rules of discipline which Mr. John Wesley promulgated in 1739. These "General Rules" are today a part of the Constitution of The Methodist Church. We still keep them officially, though it must be admitted that we have modified them in our acts and our lives as the years have gone by. This is to the distaste of many of the older Methodists who feel that we have become a soft and self-indulgent people by failing to adhere to the strict rule of the fathers. Such items as "the putting on of gold and costly apparel," have been conveniently overlooked by our people as they have become rich in this world's goods. However, it may be admitted that these rules had a meaning for people in the lower classes of Britain in 1739 which they have not today. At the time of the Wesleyan revival many such were beginning to ape and emulate the dress of the higher social classes and so getting out of their class. The same situation would hold true today were a poor person to spend more money upon clothing or ornamentation than he could afford. Mr. Wesley, who was something of a Tory himself, looked with considerable disdain upon such efforts on the part of his people.

Nevertheless, with all that, there is a sense in which Methodist discipline is at the heart of the Methodist movement. Certainly no one can read our General Rules without feeling that every sincere Christian ought to keep them in spirit if not in actual letter. Methodists so hold today—I for one do. We need more iron in our Christian blood today, as all here present will admit.

As to *orders,* there would be something of a problem in reconciling our respective theories regarding the ministry. Nevertheless some such arrangement as that which was worked out by the Episcopal Church and the Presbyterian Church regarding mutual ordination of the respective ministries might be worked out for any possible union between ourselves.

These sentences could be amplified and I will be glad to go into more detail if questions are asked.

"A"

May 7, 1951.

Both the Protestant Episcopal Church and the Methodist Church in the United States are concerned with the relationship to world fellowships of their respective communions. In the Lambeth Conference all Anglican Churches of the World have fellowship though the very term Anglican suggests a national rather than an international conference. The Methodist Ecumenical Conference brings together for consultation and cooperation all the Methodist Churches of the World.

Should the Protestant Episcopal Church and the Methodist Church in the United States unite, would the world fellowship with churches of its own communion in other lands be broken for each? If such were the case, then each church would have to decide which is the more valuable contact in the fulfillment of its mission as an agency of the Kingdom of God.

In Canada the United Church maintains contact with the world organization of each of the uniting churches—Congregational, Presbyterian, and Methodist. As illustration, the United Church of Canada elects its representatives on the Methodist Ecumenical Council and sends its delegates to the Methodist Ecumenical Conference. There is not the least difficulty in maintaining this relationship.

While a Methodist cannot speak for an Episcopalian, he can interpret the attitude of his own group. Until the World Council of Churches brings about a closer fellowship among the Protestant Churches of the World, and as long as the larger and closer world connection is between national churches of the same family, the Methodist Church would have no difficulty in uniting with another church or churches in the United States. While proposing that the United Church should maintain its connections with the world fellowship of each and all of the churches so uniting, at the

47

same time the Methodist Church realizes that the Lambeth Conference has an influence over Anglican Churches that is more authoritative than the Methodist Ecumenical Conference has over any Methodist Church.

Furthermore, Methodism has both approaches to religion. It was generally accepted at the Edinburgh Conference on Faith and Order in 1937 that the two approaches to religion made by the Churches of Christendom are the historical approach and the psychological approach. The Methodist Church has its ritual services, taken by John Wesley from the *Book of Common Prayer* of the Church of England. Some of the prayers in those services are very old and go back to earlier centuries in the history of the Christian church. Not only does Methodism lay claim to great traditions of the church through the centuries before the Reformation, but in its services it incorporates prayers that have grown out of the religious experiences of saints of other days. In a very true sense of the word, the Methodist Church is a ritualistic church and has the historical approach. On the other hand, the Methodist movement is traced to the heart-warming experience of John Wesley. Its witness is the witness to the love of God and the saving grace of our Lord, Jesus Christ. All-important is the religious experience of the believer. This is the psychological approach.

The Methodist Church does not belong to the dissenter group of churches. It would understand, therefore, why any Anglican Church would desire to keep in close touch with other Anglican Churches around the world. However, it would hope that an Anglican Church in any nation should be free to unite with any church in that nation if it should tend to strengthen the Church and hasten the union of churches into the one Church of our Lord, Jesus Christ.

CHAPTER IV

The Cornerstone of Faith*

By CHARLES D. KEAN

The Christian Church is the bearer of the Christian faith. It is not simply a continuing organization existing to promote the faith. Rather, it exists to live it, to reflect it, to bear witness to it. Just as any discussion of the Christian faith is academic if it is not also a discussion of the Christian Church through which the faith lives, so any discussion of the Christian Church is irrelevant if it is not on the basis of the Christian faith, the Church's *raison d'etre*.

The movement for organic union of the churches depends for meaning upon there being a shared awareness that there is something more significant than the merger of parallel organizations. If the reunion of the churches is to be more than a pragmatic venture, it depends upon a realized conviction on the part of the participants that the churches represent the Church at least in terms of the central Christian faith. Reunion is only possible on the basis of a community of faith which transcends in significance the differences which separate the churches.

The conviction that contact with Jesus Christ through personal commitment assures men of God's forgiveness and continuing love has been the distinctive note of the Christian religion since the days of the Apostles. To those for whom this is real, here is the conviction that the Author of all things reaches out to willful, malicious, selfish, careless men with a love made incarnate in the person of Jesus Christ which embodies the underlying purpose of creation, although it is inconceivable that any human being could earn the right to claim such consideration.

To respond to God's outreach by personal commitment to Jesus as the Lord of one's own life makes a man aware of a bond of fel-

---

* This appeared in *The Anglican Theological Review* of October, 1951.

lowship between himself and the Father, and also conscious that the walls of separation dividing him from others, and his group from other groups, have been breached. Nothing in man's nature, observed from any angle, can make this possible. It is the result of God's mercy, given to us in the person of Jesus Christ and in the continuing fellowship of those for whom He is the Lord.

In specifically modern terms, this doctrine describes accurately the human situation in every circle of human thought and action. Whether we are concerned with the contradictions of modern family life in an urban-dominated world, or with the ambiguities of the political and economic order of our day which promise so much at so high a price, or with the precarious nature of world peace in an area of atomic energy, the underlying issue is the same. Man cannot save himself, and even his good intentions turn out to be double-edged. If life is to make sense for honest, concerned people, it will only be because the love of God enables them to make sense out of it, not because human achievements eliminate human problems.

Every person with any sensitivity knows that he is capable of a far more adequate performance in his home, his business, his community, and in the wider world than he actually provides. Every person with an honesty knows that while men can and do improve situations for the better, human selfishness has a way of reappearing in the new situation, and there is no conceivable prospect of the struggle with selfishness being won for good and all. Every serious and perceptive person realizes that his own behavior, even at his noblest, entitles him to no special favor from the universe.

The Christian religion was born in a culture which was built on the insights of the Old Testament—if men only lived by the best they knew, this would be a world reflecting God's purposes, and the fellowship of such men would win the respect and emulation of mankind. The Christian religion was the result of the life, teaching, death and resurrection of Jesus Christ, showing that only a cross could fulfill the Old Testament expectation, and only the faith of those who made His cross their cross, His resurrection their resurrection, could actually meet the demands of this real world. The New Testament is the record of the faith, both of the Apostles and

the Evangelists, responding to the Gospel of our Lord Jesus Christ as the only basis for a creative relationship to God available to man.

This understanding is what the Christian Church traditionally has called "justification by faith." The term has its admitted difficulties, and is often misunderstood. It is rather unfortunate that Martin Luther's own individual reaction to the Epistle to the Romans has been enshrined in this particular phraseology in both the German and English languages. What the Christian Church is trying to say is that men are accounted as righteous by God, that men are acceptable to God, not because of their own individual or group performance in life, but through their penitent identification of themselves with Jesus Christ. Or to put it another way, New Testament Christianity is saying that more important than any opinions men hold or actions they perform is the fact that Jesus Christ serves as the lens through which God sees them and they see God, and that this is what gives hope to an otherwise frustrating life. Or in yet other words—by faith, which in itself is the gift of God, we may meet our daily problems in the confidence that God accepts us as his children, not because of our consistently good performance but because Jesus Christ lived and died and rose again among us and for us.

The doctrine of "justification by faith" is often misunderstood in the modern world, yet properly understood for what it really says it is the cornerstone of all Christian thought and action and corporate life for all time. Justification by faith in this sense makes possible the existence of the Church—it is, indeed, what makes the Church the fellowship of the sons of God. The Epistle to the Ephesians prefaces its description of the role of the Christian fellowship by stating, "By grace are we saved through faith in Christ Jesus" (Eph. 2:8). The First Epistle of St. John gives the same transforming conviction in these words, "Now we are the sons of God and it doth not yet appear what we shall be" (I John 3:2).

It is inconceivable that any religious bodies would have anything to discuss with each other besides cooperation in the areas of joint practical problems if the central conviction of "justification by faith" were not their common heritage. Except where there is a

frank recognition of this issue, what is there to unite other than groups organized for ethical and pious purposes? It is also inconceivable that branches of Christ's Church which recognize the overwhelming significance of "the mighty acts of God in Christ Jesus" for their own members in this modern world can regard other issues, no matter how important, as of equal merit. Brotherhood is first of all established on the basis of common faith, and this gives meaning to order, liturgy and church practice.

When the implications of what we have been saying are taken seriously by those interested in Christian reunion, they are committed in advance to the principle that it is the Church which is to be reunited, rather than churches which are to be merged. The Church is the necessary fellowship of those who in terms of Galatians 3:26-29 are "the children of God by faith in Christ Jesus." Without this central affirmation being first in people's thinking, it is all too easy to lose sight of the real issue—the reunion of the Church instead of the merger of the churches.

"Faith in Christ Jesus," in the light of the New Testament, is not something simply assumed to be the basis of Church life. It is the primary basis of Church worship, thought and life—and there is nothing of equal or parallel importance. The only conceivable differences between Christians, important as they may be in detail, are differences of application when it comes to relating the Gospel to the continuing life of man and society. There is nothing else of the same importance as the living conviction of men and women that through their personal contact with Jesus the Lord their fears and pride have been overcome, their forgiveness continually assured, and their fellowship with each other made an established fact.

To make anything else of absolute necessity is to deny the faith and to commit men to the heresy of "justification by works," condemned by the great Fathers of Christianity from Paul through Augustine. The marks and practices of Christian life are the reflections of the faith, they are not the same as the faith. Important for Anglicans as are the four points of the *Chicago-Lambeth Quadrilateral,* these are not on the same level as "justification by faith." Rather, they are the great traditional marks on the main

52

stream of the ongoing life of that fellowship which joins those who have "put on the new man," "which is renewed in Knowledge after the image of Him that created him; where there is neither Greek nor Jew, circumcision nor uncircumcision, Barbarian, Scythian, bond nor free, for Christ is all in all" (Colossians 3:10-11).

The Anglican Communion has always acknowledged the priority of "justification by faith," even when it recognized the real, though secondary, importance of other aspects of the Christian life. Our problem has been largely that we have tended to assume it too easily instead of continually thinking through its meaning as the cornerstone of our Church life.

The Anglican Reformation had its real origin in the recovery by the Church in England of a sense of the priority of "justification by faith" as against the medieval trend toward justification by works, in practice if not wholly in theory. The "Ten Articles" of Henry VIII, in 1536, assert the priority of justification by faith in Christ alone over matters of practice, although stating the secondary necessity of works of piety and charity. Archbishop Cranmer in his *Homily of Salvation,* in 1547, makes the dominant position of the Church of his day very clear on this subject—

Because all men be sinners and offenders against God, and breakers of his law and commandments, therefore can no man by his own acts, works and deeds (seem they ever so good) be justified and made righteous before God; but every man of necessity is constrained to seek for another righteousness, or justification, to be received at God's hands. . . . And this justification of righteousness which we receive by God's mercy and Christ's merits, embraced by faith, is taken, accepted and allowed of God for our perfect and full justification.

The Church in England included an article on "justification by faith" in the "Forty-Two Articles" of 1553. Revised in 1563 into what we now know as the "Thirty-Nine Articles," this description of the faith of the Church of England has continued to make "justification by faith" a central tenet in the Anglican understanding of Christianity. The "Thirty-Nine Articles" were enshrined in the *Book of Common Prayer* of the Protestant Episcopal Church by action of the General Convention of 1801. By action of the General Convention of 1829, the Articles were specifically included in the

deliberately cumbersome process for the amendment of the Prayer Book, as now stated in Article X of the Constitution of the Protestant Episcopal Church in the United States of America.

According to the canons of the Church of England, ordinands were required to take an oath of acceptance of the Articles from their original passage until a modification by Convocations in 1865, by which a pledge of conformity was made the substitute for an oath of acceptance. Section 3 of the Colonial Clergy Act, passed by Parliament in 1874, requires a written statement of assent—"I assent to the Thirty-Nine Articles of Religion and to the Book of Common Prayer," etc.—on the part of the colonial clergy licensed to officiate in England. Furthermore, the mutual recognition agreement attained by the Church of England and the Church of Sweden, and approved by the action of the Lambeth Conference of 1930, was on the specific assurance by the Anglican negotiators that the Church of England took seriously Article XI.

As far as there can be said to be officially formulated doctrine in a communion which is essentially Biblical as against confessional in its basic orientation, the doctrine of "justification by faith" is such a tenet. At least it must be said that the point of view which this doctrine seeks to describe is essential to main stream Anglicanism.

It is in this sense that we read the Articles of Religion, not as the Anglican parallel to the Augsburg Confession, but rather as formulations of a point of view toward reality which are passed down from generation to generation as choicest treasures of our heritage of conviction. Thus Article XI says:

We are accounted righteous before God, only for the merit of our Lord and Saviour Jesus Christ by Faith, and not for our own works or deservings. Wherefore, that we are justified by Faith only is a most wholesome Doctrine, and very full of comfort; as more largely expressed in the Homily of Justification.

Article XIX says:

The visible Church of Christ is a congregation of faithful men, in the which the pure Word of God is preached, and the Sacraments be duly

54

ministered according to Christ's ordinance, in all those things that are requisite to the same.

As the Church of Jerusalem, Alexandria and Antioch have erred; so also the Church of Rome hath erred, not only in their living and manner of ceremonies, but also in matters of Faith.

That the Church of England understands the meaning of Article XI is evidenced by the work of the great formulator of the Anglican position, Richard Hooker. In *A Learned Discourse on Justification, Works, and How the Foundation of Faith is Overthrown*, written in 1587, Hooker compares the teaching of the Church of England and the Church of Rome on precisely this point. "Justification by Faith" is called "The Foundation of Christian Doctrine" in paragraph 14, and later, referring to the Church of Rome which he exonerated from the charge of being completely unchristian, because of at least a theoretical recognition of the righteousness of Justification by Faith even though with an erroneous practice, he says, "Christian churches denying directly the foundation of Christian faith? Not directly, for then they cease to be Christian churches; but by consequent, in respect whereof we condemn as erroneous, although for holding the foundation we do and must hold them Christian" (paragraph 25).

In the *Laws of Ecclesiastical Polity,* Hooker asserts:

Not that God doth require nothing unto happiness at the hands of men saving only a naked belief (for hope and charity we may not exclude), but that without belief these other things are as nothing, and is the ground of those other divine virtues. (Book I, Chapter XI, paragraph 6.)

Again Hooker states:

Yet justified are we by faith alone, because there is neither Jew nor Gentile, nor martyr nor saint, no man whose work in whole or in part clear can make him righteous in God's sight. (Appendix to Book V.)

Anyone conversant with the history of Christian doctrine is aware that the particular issues dominant at particular periods color the way men organize and state their convictions. The doctrine of "Justification by Faith," as formulated in Anglicanism, was the sixteenth century way of recapturing a New Testament insight in terms of the essential issue of the Reformation. The Anglican reformers shared with their continental brethren the feeling that they were not creating new churches, but rather purging that section of the One, Holy, Catholic, and Apostolic Church of the heresy of "justification by works." Since the Western Catholic Church from the thirteenth century on seemed incapable of resisting this heresy through the type of organization it had developed during the Middle Ages, but rather showed over and over again that its structure and leadership not only condoned the heresy but were even heretical, Reformation was necessary.

When we approach questions of church unity in the twentieth century, it is often hard to catch the significance of battles fought in the sixteenth century, because formulae have become time-worn, brittle, misunderstood, and often empty. But it must be remembered, regardless of what we think today, that our Anglican forefathers of the sixteenth century regarded Justification by Faith as the primary issue on which the Church in England found it necessary to condemn the heresy of that part of the Church which continued to acknowledge the headship of the Pope. While Anglicans, Lutherans, and Calvinists may have differed on matters of detail, they regarded themselves as one in maintaining the New Testament orthodoxy against Roman heresy.

The twentieth century situation comes after four centuries of development of the Churches of the Reformation. It was not due to them primarily, but largely to a series of external influences—beginning with the Canons of the Council of Trent in 1559, continuing through the acts of the British Parliament in the settlement of 1688, and the effect of frontier conditions in America both on American Christianity and on the groups which sponsored evangelism on this side of the Atlantic—that the concept of denominations developed and became taken for granted as a Christian norm. This development makes it difficult for the great Churches of the Reformation to recall with practical clarity their one-time essential unity in the New Testament faith against the Roman heresy of Justification by Works. During the intervening years, they have been involved in their own conflicts against splintering movements, and they have each in their own way become marked with the effects of compromising their convictions under political pressure.

In spite of four centuries of changing conditions, however, and in spite of the rise of new problems calling for new restatements of faith in the light of particular historical circumstances, the main stream of Anglicanism has remained loyal to the essential principle of the Anglican Reformation—the priority of Justification by Faith as the cornerstone of the Church's life—and has kept with this awareness a continuing appreciation that the principle exists to be embodied and reflected in the Church's affairs. While modern statements necessarily originated as the result of modern problems, which are not precisely the same as the Reformation repudiation of the official sponsorship of heresy by the Roman curia, a sponsorship which continues to the present day, the underlying conviction can be easily discerned in the thinking of the recognized main stream leaders of modern Anglicanism.

William Temple, the late Archbishop of Canterbury, devoted Lecture XV of *Nature, Man, and God* to a discussion of Divine Grace and Human Freedom. While Archbishop Temple's Gifford Lectures are an attempt to justify the Christian orthodoxy in the intellectual climate of the 1930's rather than a specific reformulation of the sixteenth-century issue, nevertheless the essential New Testament position is clearly maintained.

This one hope, then, of bringing human selves into right relationship to God is that God should declare His love in an act, or acts, of sheer self-sacrifice, thereby winning the freely offered love of the finite selves which He has created (p. 400). All is of God; the only thing of my very own which I can contribute to my own redemption is the sin from which I need to be redeemed (p. 401). [Dr. Temple quotes as a footnote the lines from the hymn:

"Nothing in my hand I bring,
Simply to Thy Cross I cling."]

That Archbishop Temple understood the issue of the practical as well as theoretical significance of the priority of faith in real Christianity, is made clear in an earlier chapter in the same book, Lect. XII on "Revelation and Its Mode."

Faith is not the holding of correct doctrines, but personal fellowship with the living God. Correct doctrine will both express this, assist it and issue from it; incorrect doctrine will misrepresent this and hinder and prevent it. Doctrine is of an importance too great to be exaggerated, but its place is secondary, not primary. I do not believe in any creed, but I use certain creeds to express, to conserve, and to deepen my belief in God. What is offered to man's apprehension in any specific Revelation is not truth concerning God but is the living God Himself (p. 322).

The present Bishop of Derby, Dr. A. E. J. Rawlinson, in *Authority and Freedom* likewise demonstrated the same main stream of Anglican thought. In his chapter on "Evangelical Catholicism," he wrote:

It has been said that today a Catholic tendency goes through the world. It is a tendency not toward Rome but toward synthesis and unity. Let me try to put into words the vision of he Church of Christ on earth as it might be hereafter, the prophetic vision as it hovers before our eyes. The ideal, then is of a church system which shall give supremacy above all things else to the eternal Gospel of God's free grace and redemptive love in Jesus Christ, and which shall proclaim the primacy of the two great commandments of love towards God and of love towards man; a Church system, therefore, which shall be genuinely evangelical and free; at the same time a Church system which shall comprise within itself, held together in a free and lasting synthesis and genuinely penetrated by the inner spirit of the Gospel, those various elements of institutional and sacramental religion, of popular religious custom and devotional practice and spiritual mysticism, of moral discipline and of intellectual thought, which do not directly flow from the Gospel itself, but which nevertheless form part of the historic inheritance of Christianity (pp. 183f.).

A third contemporary scholar, like Dr. Temple and Dr. Rawlinson enjoying a reputation above all lines of Church party, demonstrates the same essential point of view. In *The Grace of God in Faith and Philosophy,* Canon Leonard Hodgson, Regius Professor of Divinity at Oxford, dealt with the perennial problem of Pelagianism within the Church. He understood the underlying issue of the Reformation in much the same way as has been stated in this study, and likewise pointed out the danger of transforming the New Testament understanding of faith and love into an externalized *thing,* as much a form of Justification by Works as medieval sacramentalism. He writes:

Both Catholicism and Protestantism wish to bear witness to three positive truths: (1) Man's salvation is God's gift, freely given through the crucified and risen Christ. (2) Man's relation to God is a personal and ethical relation. This truth would be corrupted by any view which thought of man being 'mechanically' or 'physically' saved irrespective of his own personal character. (3) Being God's free gift, salvation is not in any sense earned by man or received as a reward for merit (p. 3).

Again Canon Hodgson writes:

The attempt to safeguard personal moral responsibility by a doctrine of merit is the first step towards the degradation of Catholicism; the better way is by the doctrine of justification by faith. The doctrine of justification by faith needs safeguarding against Pelagianism, and Catholic sacramentalism rightly understood will here give Protestantism help where it needs it most. Let us take first the doctrine of justification by faith. It is by faith that man lays hold on the forgiveness offered by God in Christ and is restored to his true life of growth in communion with God. This faith expresses itself in acknowledgment of sinfulness and impotence, in personal loyalty to Christ and reliance upon Him for strength to serve Him. This faith is both the expression of the man's own free response to the love of God shown forth in Christ, and also God's gift through which the man responds (p. 170).

As Canon Theodore O. Wedel maintains, in *The Coming Great Church,*

The ultimate problem of religion is the problem of the Divine-Human Encounter. It is the problem of bridging the gulf between holy divine love and human guilt. The Gospel is the drama of that bridging. Christ is the final Mediator. The Church is built on that Faith. The central doctrine of the Reformation, Justification by Faith, seized upon this insight. This doctrine has been misinterpreted often, but the whole Bible supports it. The essential meaning of it is that the gulf between man and God has been crossed. Christ's work has been accomplished. No further sacrifice is needed except the sacrifice of praise and thanksgiving. No good works are needed except as they are a necessary response to the acceptance, in penitence and faith, of the unearned love of God (p. 98). . . . The first step toward a united people of God is the rediscovery of our common heritage in basic Apostolic faith (p. 119).

While the foregoing citations can hardly be regarded as an exhaustive survey of the subject, they indicate, nevertheless, that representative Anglican thinkers, acknowledged as such by all major groups within the Anglican Communion, have appreciated the primacy of New Testament faith in all questions of Christian thought and action. The original Anglican Reformers dealt with the problem of their age from this point of view, and the Anglican statesmen of the twentieth century are dealing with problems which arise out of the circumstances of our age, yet the basic understanding is the same.

But while justification by faith has always been central in main stream Anglican thinking, it has tended to be taken for granted since the passing of the original Reformation conflict, except when someone like Canon Hodgson deliberately deals with the same subject matter. It is certainly true that this central affirmation has not been given the attention it ought to have received in those circles interested in Christian reunion, where it has generally been assumed to be accepted without its implications for Christian reunion being worked through systematically. The Anglican conferees who negotiated the agreement with the Church of Sweden were faced with this issue, but the establishment of intercommunion took place without the opportunity offered being used by the entire Anglican Communion to think through its central affirmation explicitly. The recent suggestion of the Bishop of Madura, Dr. J. E. L. Newbiggin, that justification by faith is the first issue to be considered in questions of reunion (*The Reunion of the Church,* VI) has yet to receive the serious attention it deserves. Although Dr. Newbiggin came to the South India episcopate from the Presbyterian tradition, he is, as a matter of fact, suggesting nothing which would be strange to Anglican ears.

It is not enough to pay lip service to the insights of the New Testament and to assume that everybody either knows what he means or what he says when he subscribes to a great traditional doctrine like Justification by Faith. It is possible that the cause of Christian reunion has been retarded by the fact that negotiators have so often tended to assume that they were "one in the faith" by agreeing to verbalisms. Perhaps they have been precisely one in the faith, but the very process of discovering the fact would establish the relative significance of other issues—since no tradition

THE CORNERSTONE OF FAITH

can have any value in Christian thought and practice whatsoever if it is distinctly at variance with the central faith itself.

While there is room certainly for variant emphases and customs within the larger Church, it is impossible for those who hold to the faith of the New Testament to compromise with any tradition which suggests or implies works as necessary for salvation. Church order and discipline, worship and sacrament are to be considered as means by which the central faith is appreciated, expressed, interpreted, strengthened, focussed, sharpened, and made available in the continuing life of the Christian fellowship.

Questions of the significance of tradition of this type, which are of proven value in human experience age after age, have to be approached from the standpoint of the Gospel, not vice versa. But regardless of any values accruing from subscription to either the necessity of baptism by immersion, as held by American Southern Baptists, or acknowledgment of the Roman Pontiff as head of the Church on earth, as held by the Roman Catholics, these doctrines are heretical in that they are a form of justification by works. Christians, who are loyal to the New Testament faith, can discuss all sorts of questions of real but secondary importance, provided that all the discussants are clear as to what they mean by their common appreciation of justification by faith as the "foundation of the Church," to use Hooker's term. They have nothing whatever to discuss with those who make some form of works prior, or equivalent, either overtly or by implication, to faith in Christ Jesus as all-sufficient for our salvation.

We shall rejoice greatly, when in the Province of God, extremists on both sides of the central New Testament faith are led to repent so that we may converse in the same language. It is not that Anglicans and others who are loyal to the Doctrine of Justification by Faith are sinless themselves, but that this central doctrine can only be compromised at the expense of the Church itself ceasing to be a Church in a New Testament sense, so that the result of compromise, even if it leads to organic union, is in the nature of a political merger rather than the knitting together of the Body of Christ.

As we approach negotiations with Christian groups which, like ourselves, subscribe to the New Testament faith, although its six-teenth-century articulation may have been by different people in somewhat different words, we know that the clarification of our central convictions by discussion of these directly, instead of taking them for granted, will establish that spirit of brotherhood in the faith which will make it possible to deal with real differences on the level of sacrament and order with charity and understanding. In making this suggestion, we are not making any innovation at all, but are making available for Anglican participation in the ecumenical movement the main stream of the faith as our communion has always held it.

CHAPTER V

The Christian Ministry

By ROBERT F. GIBSON, JR.

In the opinion of this writer a clear understanding, a clear doctrine of the ministry *is still unfolding* in history under the guidance of God the Holy Spirit. We, indeed, are serious participants in this unfolding. This does not mean that something new is yet to be created. From the days of the earthly ministry of Jesus Christ there has always been a Christian ministry, and from the divine point of view it must be clear what is its nature, function and power. But what Christian men have not commonly and universally received and accepted any one doctrine of the ministry is obvious.

Such a thesis should not be surprising and is not unusual. It is rather but one example of the way the Holy Spirit works and reveals God in history. Christian doctrines have been received and accepted only through long historical process. No matter how determinative and "once for all" God's mighty acts may be, men manifestly need unfolding guidance in time before they clearly see such divine gifts. This process never stops: "We see through a glass darkly"; God, even in Christ, is "veiled in flesh"; but God the Spirit "will guide us into all truth."

Certain doctrines, however, did become clear in the past, and Christians have universally taken them as being given once for all. The Bible is our outstanding example of this. It is difficult for us to realize but time was when Christian men had no Bible in our settled sense of the word. This is not to say there was no word of God until the Council of Carthage in the year A.D. 397 God spoke through many men and many writings, and was heard, but finally the day came when certain writings were accepted and since then Christians have had the Bible. In like manner the

Nicene and Apostles' Creeds were centuries in forming and more in finding general Christian acceptance, but this surely is not to say there was no substance of the faith in the mighty acts of God until that happy day. A further example of the unfolding of doctrine in history under the guidance of the Holy Spirit is seen in the so-called Ecumenical Councils. Surely God the Holy Spirit is present in all councils "where two or three or met together" in the name of Jesus Christ, but men do not necessarily hear or heed His voice. Only with centuries of living Christian experience, only with hindsight, has the Church singled out four particular Councils and accepted in a truly universal way their doctrinal findings as of the authority of the Holy Ghost.

These three, Bible, Creed and Councils, outstanding examples, are the embodiment of living Christian experience under the guidance and teaching of the Holy Spirit. All came into existence gradually, were judged by the Church's experience with them, were then accepted as divine revelation, and finally were preserved and communicated. In a broader way, following the same principle, one can point out that the Church of the Apostolic Age did not know, say or do what the Church of the Classical Period knew, said and did, nor the Church of the Middle Ages, nor the Modern, nor the Post-Modern new age. Each had errors in what was said and done, each devised new forms and methods, but each continued the historic faith and *understood more of God's truth through the Holy Spirit when experience had made such understanding possible.*

It is the thesis of this paper that the Christian Ministry can, indeed should, be viewed in this same light. Just as the visible Ecumenical Church of which we dream is still in the future by this process, so the ecumenical ministry is subject to the same process. While certain groups or communions of Christians assume, and believe, that they have the true ministry, or hold the true doctrine of the ministry, still nothing is clearer than the manifest divisions in Christendom on this very subject. When one admits, however, that in Anglicanism and in Methodism there is something new under the guidance of the Holy Spirit, just as there is in the contemporary Ecumenical Movement, and as there

64

was in the Reformation or in the Western Papal Church or in the Infant Catholic Church of the second to fifth centuries as compared to the Church of the Apostolic Age, then one admits the possibility of unfolding revelation regarding the Church's ministry. As facts of development and change enter into the scene of the Visible Church, then attendant development and change takes place in the doctrine of the ministry, whether officially or unofficially. Indeed a Doctrine of the Church appears as primary with a doctrine of the ministry always dependent upon it.

This is not to say that a *new ministry* is created any more than that a *new church* is created. It is to say that new circumstances and experience necessitate new form, and new explanation and justification of that form. Such is the history of Christian Doctrine and the history of the Visible Church and the history of the Visible Ministry. It is still true and we are involved in it today.

1. *What Do We Know From History?*

Origins and Apostolic Fathers—One is on dangerous ground indeed when he attempts to be definitive about the early ministry. The ablest scholars are at odds in their handling of the material whether it be the New Testament or other primitive evidence. It seems clear that the evidence to date provides no *conclusive* answers on the origin or nature or form of the ministry. It is therefore dangerous, at least, to base definite doctrine upon it.

Modern scholarship, however, emboldens one to draw some conclusions which can be based on present agreement between leading writers of diverse background and schools of thought. Some such conclusions follow:

1) The three-fold ministry of bishops, priests and deacons in its developed Anglican form is not present in the first century, though all of its functions may well be present.

2) There is continuity of Church from Christ and the Apostles, but there is no general agreement as to "what it depends on." This continuity was widely denied a generation behind us but the fact is now accepted by non-episcopal scholars.

3) New Testament names, in the main, represent functions, and there is development in form and in formal terminology.

65

4) Eucharistic officers represent the origin of the developed forms. This was demonstrated by the Protestant scholar, Rudolph Sohm, in the nineteenth century and is clearly supported and promoted by such scholars as Dom Gregory Dix today.

5) Jesus Christ did give the Apostolic group a commission which passed through some kind of succession to the later episcopate. On the positive side there is this much of a general acceptance of the traditional Catholic view. But there is far from general agreement that this was the *only method of continuity*.

After stating these five general conclusions it should be noted that the world of non-Roman Christian scholarships has taken a long time and a great many books in getting this much agreement regarding the ministry in the Primitive Church. The conclusions have been arrived at by a dialectical process through the years between Protestant and Catholic scholars. Both have been necessary. Modifications and concessions have been made on each side due to opposing scholarly pressure. The conclusions, simple as they may appear, could hardly have been reached without the give and take of Protestant vs. Catholic attempts to justify respectively inherited positions.

Subsequent History—The history of the Christian ministry might roughly be divided into three general periods with a fourth period now beginning to take shape.

First: The period of origins and development can be extended to about the year A.D. 500, by which time all diverse forms have been absorbed, or lost to history, and doctrines of episcopacy and priesthood have taken shape.

Second: There is the long span of so-called Middle Ages of more than one thousand years in which there is a practically universal episcopate with its own succession by laying-on-of-hands and the lesser ministries authorized by episcopal ordination. Disagreement of practice or theory appears at three major points in this period:

1) Disagreement on the person and powers of the chief bishop, the pope;

2) Disagreement on some functions of the episcopate other than the ordaining function: This disappeared rather early as the papal

66

pattern became established, and was largely confined to the Irish Church and its missions;

3) Disagreement as to the number of "orders" of the ministry whether two or three or seven, with the major difference being whether the episcopate is a separate order from the priesthood (Rome maintaining that it is not).

Third: There is the period of approximately four centuries since the Reformation. This was a time of experimentation *through historical necessity* producing several general forms of ministry, most obviously differentiated by the means and source of authorization. Four such forms can be noted:

1) Individualistic type resulting from what is felt to be a direct personal call and authorization;

2) Congregationally authorized;

3) Ordained by Presbyters;

4) Ordained by Bishops. There is the additional variant where there is ordination by bishops but after a break in historic episcopal continuity, which represents a kind of combination between the third and fourth forms. It should be noted that these classifications do not attempt to describe a self-understanding of the various forms, for the meaning of the ministry becomes clear only in terms of the life of each particular church.

Such is roughly the outline of the history of the ministry. In the last half century, however, there appears to be the beginning of a new period. Out of the experience, good and bad, of the nineteen hundred years of Christian living, there is a growing attempt to reconcile the developed differences. Along with the dream of a truly Ecumenical Church is the necessary dream of a universal ministry. This brings us to the present.

Present Views—As in the historical sketch above, some approximation of current views may be attempted with the recognition that both authority and knowledge are wanting when one speaks for others. It appears that in the Eastern Orthodox Communion "The Church" is that which is essential with the ministry within the Church. Some of their modern theologians even argue (e.g.: Bulgakov) that the Church creates the hierarchy. The trouble with all the rest of us and our ministries is that we are apostates.

The Roman Catholic view is similar in that their orders are valid because it is the true Church, and schism from the true Church invalidates all other orders. Historic continuity of orders is stressed, however. Rome would never say "the Church creates the hierarchy" but would come nearer to saying that by authority from St. Peter and his successors the hierarchy is constitutive of the Church.

The general Protestant view, though each group might attempt to justify its particular form, would appear to be that whatever break in continuity or form took place at the Reformation or later, it was either a return to primitive purity, or (and far more logically) it was divinely sanctioned and used. The new means and source of authorization for ministries breaking from the fifteen hundred years continuity was, to put it simply, inspired and empowered by God the Holy Spirit.

This would appear to be an extension of the affirmation of John the Baptist when he said "God is able to raise up from these stones children unto Abraham." Of course God is able to do what He will. He did make children unto Abraham out of Gentiles, and He did use and bless ministries apart from historic succession. Perhaps it is worth paraphrasing here the remark of a noted scholar of the Church of England, Dr. Leonard Hodgson, when he said, "Where in non-episcopal ministries God apparently raised men to do the work neglected or obstructed by bishops, it certainly ill becomes Episcopalians to doubt those ministers or their sacraments."

The Anglican View—An Anglican view of the ministry is probably the most difficult to expound even for a member of that communion. There are evident reasons for this difficulty. The Anglican Communion, of which the Protestant Episcopal Church in the U.S.A. is an integral part, bound by voluntary but profound ties, is not a Confessional Church and does not officially subscribe to propositional theology. This means that it does not have, and really cannot have in loyalty to itself, dogmatic propositions regarding the ministry. Time and again its bishops in Lambeth have refused to accept any particular definition of the Historic Episcopate to the exclusion of others.* This seeming weakness is in reality the firm ground of sticking to fact. It does not pretend to know that which has not been clearly revealed; but it does staunchly and faithfully adhere to that ministry, and its means of perpetuation, which from the earliest observable times has been the ministry of the Holy Catholic Church and with which it has unbroken continuity.

This leads to a second difficulty. The Anglican Communion has its continuity through the Church of England, which historically was a National church presuming its right to legislate regarding the ministry functioning within its National borders. It did not have the right, or assume it, to legislate regarding the Christian ministry in general, or the ministry in any other nation's territory. This historic fact has greatly confused the issue, however, since the Church of England has planted its off-spring in many other lands, and since in that land itself there is no longer National adherence to the one-church concept. Those who depend on English Church heritage are now in a totally different situation and cannot rightly use the same basis in defending a particular form of ministry. This has misled both the insiders and outsiders. There has never been a church speaking for the United States of America, and therefore Episcopalians fall either into the realm of denominational rights and authority or into that of the Holy Catholic Church's rights and authority. Confusion abounds when they speak to either from the now non-existent English position. Anglicanism (not its Mother Church or its ministry, but rather its international communion aspect) is something new, almost precisely the same age as Methodism. It is not the Church of England. England and its Church History, therefore, cannot be determinative for Anglicanism, however valuable, influential, or informative they may be.

There is still another, and indeed a crucial, difficulty in expounding an Anglican view of the ministry. Anglican uniqueness in Christendom is its Reformed-Catholic nature. It is a living paradox. One must see its two sides to find its truth and to know

* See: Report of Lambeth Conference, 1920.

its power. The subsequent tension, which is the tension of world-wide Christianity (Protestant vs. Catholic) was more readily held in balance in a national Church. Anglicans in this country tend to the *either* "protestant" *or* "catholic," so that the Episcopal Church often *appears* to the outsider to be two different bodies united by some mysterious bond. Out of this situation attitudes toward the ministry tend to fall into these same categories to the great confusion of the outsider, and sometimes to the insider as well. Here again, however, apparent weakness is the real strength. The Anglican Communion and its ministry have a comprehensive, "both and" nature which may be of definite value to a divided Christendom.

Inside the Communion, and partly at least because of the "both and" tensions, Anglicans have indulged themselves in debate as to whether the Historic Episcopate is of the "esse" or the "bene esse" of the Church. Is it "essential" or does it pertain to the "well being" of the Church only? This is here mentioned precisely for the avoidance of such debate on the outside. It has not in the opinion of this writer, proved fruitful. One never knows enough about the "essence" of the Church (other than that it is Christ) to conclude the debate. It is like the case of a man born blind and a debate as to whether eyesight is essential to man or only to his well-being. Although man would never have been man without eyes, still particular men have been very human indeed without them, in spite of that which was lacking in their well-being. This seems to be the dilemma in which the debate always rests, and it might better be left there.

Anglicans are staunchly agreed, however, that the Historic Episcopate, and ordination through continuous succession from earliest times, is essential to Anglicanism. All recognize in this aspect of Apostolic Succession, at least, something so valuable that they cannot foresee the possibility of forsaking it. Why? Can one explain without dogmatizing, without doing what the Communion has officially been unwilling to do?

2. *Looking Toward a Doctrine*

It would appear that *continuity* is intimately related to *universality* in matters of Christian doctrine. The basic factor is, of course, the Godgivenness. But teaching about the acts of God, that which is subject to human judgment, becomes universalized through continuity. All churches and all ministries obviously have continuous elements from Jesus Christ through some kind of succession. Contrariwise, it is precisely the individual revelation or teaching or authorization, whether of person or group, which is not universally accepted by Christians. God acts, God reveals, and continuity from that act achieves general acceptance.

This would apply to the Two Sacraments, to the Bible and to the Historic Creeds. It appears to apply in like manner to the Historic Ministry. This Anglicanism seems to be saying in the *Chicago-Lambeth Quadrilateral.** Anglicanism is one with Orthodoxy and Rome in recognizing these four continuous and universal elements (although one must acknowledge the serious divisions about the nature of particular successions). It is also one with general Protestantism in recognizing the first three of these. And, while there can obviously be no universally authorized ministry until there is a universally recognized Church, the continuity factor in the ministry would clearly appear to be necessary to its general acceptance.

This is far more than political expedience. It is so definitely the lesson Christian history, paralleling other universal elements, that one may safely assume divine guidance and teaching. Other ministries, however blessed and fruitful they have been, have lacked the universal factor *with whatever it contains of power and authority.*

This continuity factor, with its value, power and authority, however, is manifestly not exclusively or finally determinative. It is not Protestantism alone which would demonstrate this. Rome and Orthodoxy testify to the same principle when insisting that schism or apostacy invalidate even continuous episcopal orders. Something more then is needed in addition to historic and continuous succession. The ministries of East and West were mutually challenged after the historic break over the papacy. The right ministry thus early appears as that which represents the right

* See: Statement on Faith and Order, General Convention, Protestant Episcopal Church. 1949.

71

Church. Regardless of the arguments between Rome and Constantinople, or their soundness, the principle here involved appears valid and is substantiated by subsequent Christian history, as well as by that of the earlier formative period. Church and ministry are inescapably bound together. Thus history would teach us that the ministry must be *faithful* as well as *continuous,* or God will raise up those who challenge and correct that the Church may be His, not man's.

From earliest times the bishop was recognized as, and supposed to be: Chief Pastor, Defender of the Faith, Chief Missionary, Center of Sacramental Life, Channel of Succession, and Symbol of Authority. It might be simply observed that when bishops, or the ministry in general, grossly neglected or distorted these functions then, in the course of time, others were moved to assume them. When ministers usurped God's authority, when the faith was distorted or ignored, when sacraments were neglected or abused, when the Word of God was withheld and mediators of God's grace became barriers, or shepherds acted like wolves, something happened. This is not alone the story of the late Middle Ages; it can be observed in part in every age, from the Hebrew prophets, down to the present time.

Continuity of ministry has proved to be a great safeguard. Thus all types of ministry tend to set up forms of continuous succession. But continuity is ever in danger of idolizing itself, thus blocking the spirit and forgetting the faith for which it exists. A process of check and balance has shown itself through the centuries and appears necessary to the ministry. The best of illustrations can be found in the English Church heritage. In the sixteenth century revolt against Medieval distortions and neglect changed many aspects of the church and ministry, but historic continuity preserved many essentials which were lost in other Reformation movements. But, when the catholic but reformed ministry of England neglected the power and the voice of the Spirit in individual lives, Quakerism arose. Later when the Episcopal ministry neglected its true missionary and evangelical purpose at home and abroad Methodism arose. Then when that ministry neglected certain catholic elements of its heritage, particularly its sacramental

72

emphases, the Oxford movement arose. Still later when true shepherding of outcasts was neglected the Salvation Army arose.

All this with what results? The Oxford Movement produced only minor schism with some few laity and clergy turning from the Church of England to the Orthodox and Roman communions. To the enrichment of the ministry and the strengthening of the church the movement remained to be an inside corrective. But when Quakerism and Salvation Army cut themselves off, or were excluded from historic continuity, they were mortally weakened. Others more competent than this writer can speak for Methodism, but surely there are elements of loss clear to that body despite continuing missionary success. And, Anglicanism is weak or incomplete in direct relation to these movements of faith and spirit apart from its communion and historic ministry.

This English illustration could be multiplied many times throughout the stream of Christian experience by observing the check and balance of ministry and faith, one might also say of body and spirit, as history unfolds. It remains to gather from this scene those lessons of history which appear to describe the true qualities of the Christian Ministry. Some, at least, are as follows:

1) The ministry has continuity, not alone from Christ and His Apostles, but also from that developed form in which, like the Creeds, it achieved universal acceptance.

2) It is a ministry of the Word, preaching, evangelizing, ever missionary in its purpose.

3) It is a ministry of the sacraments.

4) It upholds the faith as received in Bible and Creeds, and takes leadership in guarding that faith.

5) It recognizes and shares a priesthood of all believers, never conceiving itself as the only channel of Christian grace, or finding its own sufficiency apart from a responsible laity.

6) It should be shepherd and pastor to men of every race and class.

7) It should recognize the freedom of the Holy Spirit to speak and to use men, and hear in voices outside the ministry the God-given check upon its human limitations.

8) It should exercise its authority as derived from the whole Church.

In broad outline these are the elements of thesis and antithesis which have caused Christian schism and produced rival ministries, yet most elements tend to reappear in any Christian group with a long life span. A true synthesis would thus appear to be the goal toward which the ministry is being led. As Christians strive for a united Church it would seem clear that they should take with them in the future all that the Holy Spirit has revealed through the past as pertaining to His truth and His power. That such may come to pass is surely our united Christian prayer.

CHAPTER VI

The Ministry in the Methodist Church

By DANIEL L. MARSH

The Methodist Church, in common with all Christian churches, recognizes that ministers are necessary for the welfare, and indeed the existence, of the Church. The report which "The Joint Commission on Approaches to Unity" submitted to the General Convention of the Protestant Episcopal Church in 1949 contains a paragraph on "The Ministry" which is as true for the Methodist Church as it is for the Episcopal Church. The statement is as follows: "Christ supplies the Church, of which He is the living Head, with a ministry continuous through the centuries and empowered by the Holy Spirit to proclaim the Word and administer the Sacraments. The Church thankfully receives this ministry and through it exercises the prophetic, priestly and pastoral functions committed to the Church by its Lord."

The evangelical revival which was conducted by John and Charles Wesley was a revival of essential Protestantism. The Protestant Reformation itself was an attempt to recapture the genius, the spirit, and the passion of the Christianity of the first two or three centuries. John Wesley was a mountain-minded man. He knew from his profound study of the New Testament that the Christian religion does not consist in rites and ceremonies or in mere intellectual assent to creedal dogma. He knew that essential Christianity is experience and life. Stern logician though he was, yet he knew that life was larger than logic. You will find the quintessence of the Protestant Reformation and the essentials of early Christianity in everything that John Wesley did. Since this paper has to do only with the ministry, we limit ourselves to that single subject.

The Protestant reformers renounced the entire Roman Catholic hierarchy of cardinals, archbishops, bishops, and parish priests set apart and elevated by the sacrament of ordination, in which they assumed that they were endowed by special powers and prerogatives as the reputed successors of the Apostles. The reformers showed that this hierarchy did not exist in the early Christian Church. The New Testament makes it clear that all members of the Christian Church are called to be Christ's witnesses and instruments in the spread of His Kingdom. At the same time, the early Church recognized the necessity of setting apart certain of its members for special work, such as the preaching of the Word and the administering of the Sacraments. There was at first no such thing as an hierarchical system consisting of three orders as the orders of deacons, elders, and bishops are conceived of today, and no one Bishop was supreme over the others. Let us look at the unfolding and developing of the orders of the ministry.

Early in the history of the Christian Church there were plainly two orders, deacons and elders. The deacon served tables; assisted the elders; was allowed to baptize, and doubtlessly assisted the elders in the Holy Communion. The order above the diaconate was the elder—and there was nothing higher in the early Church. The elder was authorized and empowered to perform all the prophetic and priestly functions of the ministry. In the Greek, an elder was called a *presbyteros*. Perhaps he was so called because it was the custom, even in the Jewish economy, to make the older men the responsible leaders, and hence he was called an elder.

This word *presbyteros* is a fine illustration of the romance of words. Look at it: First the elder, or person in charge of a Christian congregation, was called in the Greek language a *presbyteros*. Then among the Latins, he was called a *presbyter*. When Christianity was carried to the British Isles, the Anglo-Saxons reduced *presbyter* to *preost,* much as modern college students reduce "professor" to "prof." By the time English became the dominant language of Britain, *preost* became "priest," and so we designate him to this day.

At first, every Christian congregation had a *presbyter* in charge, and sometimes several *presbyters*. As the movement spread, and congregations increased in number and in size, the early Chris-

76

THE MINISTRY IN THE METHODIST CHURCH

tains felt that it was desirable to pick one of the elders out and make him a supervisor or overseer of the work of the congregation. Naturally they would pick out the most dynamic and aggressive leader among the *presbyters*. This one they called an overseer, which in the Greek language was made up of two words, *epi,* meaning "over," and *skopos,* meaning "a seer" or "inspector." Hence an *episkopos* was "an overseer." When this *episkopos* or "overseer" got into the Latin, he was called *episcopus.* When he got among the Anglo-Saxons, who never liked long words, they reduced the episcopus to *bisceop* and then *biscop,* and finally the English called him "bishop."

Now keep in mind that every congregation had one or more bishops, howsoever many congregations there might be, and howsoever little and insignificant they might be. It was natural that the *presbyters,* or overseers, or bishops in charge of the larger congregations should become more influential than those of the smaller parishes. It was this way that archbishops finally developed: the bishops in charge of the Churches at such places as Jerusalem, Antioch, Ephesus, Alexandria, Constantinople, and Rome became the best known and the most influential; but they were all equal in power. No one had any authority over any other one during the first couple of centuries. Toward the end of the third century, the prestige of Rome as the capital of the world enhanced the prestige of the bishop of the Church at Rome. Moreover Rome was the one Church in the west that was of apostolic origin, and that seemed to lend it increasing significance as time passed.

Saint Paul was definitely identified with the Church at Rome. Saint Peter's name is traditionally attached to it also. There is no sure historical evidence that Peter was ever in Rome, but there is a persistent tradition to that effect. I incline toward the acceptance of the tradition; but even then there is no evidence that he was ever bishop of the Church at Rome. However, what if he had been? He was also bishop of the Church at Antioch. In the parlance of present day slang, "so what?"

We also recall the New Testament account of how Jesus once asked His Disciples for their appraisement of Him. Peter, in a

77

luminous moment of inspiration and enthusiasm, blurted out a memorable utterance in which he revealed a profound knowledge of the nature of Jeus: "Thou art the Christ, the Son of the living God." Jesus was pleased with His ardent Disciple's prompt and unwavering devotion. Then, making symbolic use of the surname (a "stone") which he had bestowed upon Peter, He eulogized him, speaking in words so obviously figurative and emotional that they can be twisted into meaning almost anything that a partisan wishes them to mean: "Thou art Peter, and upon this rock I will build my church. . . . I will give unto thee the keys of the Kingdom of Heaven."

Whatever else these words may mean, one thing is certain: Jesus, who had combatted the priestcraft of His day even unto death, did not intend to build up a new priestcraft more dominant than the old. Origen, one of the Church fathers, insists that the promise was made not to Peter alone but to every disciple who joins in Peter's confession. Saint Chrysostom holds that the rock was not Peter but Peter's faith, "the faith of his confession." Christ delivered the "keys of the Kingdom" to all the apostles as much as to Peter. The whole imagery is one of discipline, and it naturally passed from the apostles to the Church rather than from one man to his alleged successors.

All of the foregoing is to be kept in mind when we study the ministry from the Methodist point of view. John and Charles Wesley stood in the true apostolic evangelistic succession. They had a revolutionary experience kindered to that which had been recorded by Paul, Augustine, Luther, and Bunyan. Early in his ministry, John Wesley visited Herrnhut, near Dresden, which contained about a thousand devout Moravians, the people who so profoundly influenced him on his missionary journey to Georgia. In reporting his visit, Wesley says that the Moravians "hold fast the faith and practice of the Apostolic Church."

All of the foregoing lies back of the conception of the ministry as held by John Wesley not only, but also by the Methodist Church as a whole.

New Testament Christianity used lay preachers. So did Wesley, and so does Methodism in this day, especially in Britain and

Ireland. John Wesley had a strong sense of Anglican Church propriety. Therefore, he was on the point of censuring a young layman, Thoman Maxfield, for preaching to London Methodists. When his mother, Susannah, by that time a widow, heard of this, she counseled Wesley as follows: "Take care what you do with respect to that young man, for he is as surely called of God to preach as you are. Examine what have been the fruits of his preaching, and hear him also yourself." That was the beginning. From then on, Wesley used laymen more and more as class leaders, as exhorters, as local preachers. They are still used, but the *Discipline of the Methodist Church* (Paragraph 302) specifically states that "no members of the church shall be at liberty to preach without a license."

Of course, Wesley as a person believed and the Methodist Church as an institution believes in a ministry set apart for full-time service to the Church and the Kingdom of God. The Methodists have always believed in "the call to preach." This "call" is not the coinage of ideal desire nor some "bodiless creation ecstasy." It bears the stamp of common sense which John Wesley was wont to put on everything, as is revealed in Paragraph 301 of the *Discipline,* which deals with "the call to preach," thus:

"In order that we may try those persons who profess to be moved by the Holy Spirit to preach, let the following questions be asked, namely:

"1. Do they know God as a pardoning God? Have they the love of God abiding in them? Do they desire nothing but God? Are they holy in all manner of conversation?

"2. Have they gifts, as well as grace, for the work? Have they a clear, sound understanding; a right judgment in the things of God; a just conception of salvation by faith? Do they speak justly, readily, clearly?

"3. Have they fruit? Have any been truly convinced of sin and converted to God, and are believers edified by their preaching?

"As long as these marks concur in anyone, we believe he is called of God to preach. These we receive as sufficient proof that he is moved by the Holy Spirit."

Naturally, Wesley believed in orders, and so does the Methodist Church today. The present *Discipline* (Paragraphs 392 and 393) states that "a deacon is constituted by the election of the Annual Conference and the laying on of the hands of a bishop. A deacon

79

has authority to preach, to conduct divine worship, to perform the marriage ceremony, to administer Baptism, and to assist an elder in administering the Lord's Supper." It further states (Paragraphs 401 and 402) that "an elder is constituted by the election of the Annual Conference, and by the laying on of hands of a bishop and of elders. An elder has authority to preach, to conduct divine worship, to administer the Sacraments of Baptism and the Lord's Supper, and to perform the marriage ceremony."

John Wesley believed that there were only two orders, deacons and elders,—or *presbyters*. In Ireland this past summer, I came across an "Agreed Statement on the significance of Ordination received by the General Assembly of the Presbyterian Church and the Irish Conference of the Methodist Church in 1944," which seems like a fair statement of the subject. It is as follows: "Ordination is the public recognition of gifts of ministry and the giving of authority for their exercise. This authority is derived not from those already ordained, but from the whole body of the faithful in each denomination, and ultimately from God, working through them. Ordination sets the seal of the whole Church on men of approved piety and gifts, dedicates them to God and commends them to all men as approved ministers of Jesus Christ."

It is easy for Methodism today, with precedent and the riches of research scholarship at its disposal, to believe in only two orders. It was brave and penetrating scholarship on the part of Wesley that made him so believe. The belief was put into practice by Wesley to meet the exigencies of the situation created among his followers in America by the Revolutionary War.

Both of Wesley's grandfathers had been non-conformist preachers; but his father and mother had returned to the Anglican Church, and his father had become a rather narrow Anglican. John and Charles Wesley both belonged to the Anglican Communion, believed in it, and defended it. Charles Wesley requested that when he died, he be buried in ground consecrated by the Anglican Church. But when John Wesley died, he was buried back of City Road Chapel, which he himself had built, the mother church of world-wide Methodism. When some Anglican visited Wesley's grave, and asked, "Who consecrated this ground?", the proper answer was made by a devout follower of Wesley, "The bones of the holy man buried here have consecrated it forever."

At the beginning of his ministry Wesley was such a martinet for churchmanship, such a devotee of the clerical proprieties, that he was reluctant and slow to undertake outdoor preaching. He finally entered upon what became a tremendous outdoor preaching program only because he could in this way reach sinful men and women who would not enter any church to hear the Gospel. As Wesley went on, he became infinitely more concerned about apostolic success than he was about apostolic succession, and his *Journal* is replete with miracles of redemption wrought as a result of his preaching. When the church at Epworth, where his father had long been the rector, denied John Wesley the right to preach from the pulpit, John mounted the tombstone over his father's grave, and preached to the neighbors who crowded about to hear him. When preachers of the Church of England objected to Wesley preaching in their respective parishes, Wesley replied that the world was his parish. Another time when a bishop forbade him to enter a certain parish, Wesley replied that he would obey God rather than man, and went in and preached. He was more than once threatened with excommunication, but good sense finally prevailed, and he was never driven out of the Church.

The same independence, resourcefulness and self-reliance characterized Wesley when he was confronted with the necessity of supplying ordained ministers to administer the Sacraments to his followers in America. Wesley had been sending ministers to America before the Revolution, and they had been highly successful. However, when the American Revolution broke out, the English preachers all returned to England, excepting only Francis Asbury. Francis Asbury stayed and, with the American Methodist lay preachers, wrought mightily, and became one of the greatest props of the new nation whose moral foundations he so valiantly and faithfully helped to lay. But Asbury was not at the time of the Revolution an ordained minister, and so the Methodist flock was left without anybody to administer the Sacraments. They appealed to Wesley. The spiritual needs of the American Methodists had been in Wesley's thoughts all through the Revolutionary

81

War. A few weeks after the ratification of the Treaty of Peace, he sent a letter "to the preachers in America," approving of Asbury's leadership. Then Wesley went to Dr. Lowth, Bishop of London, and asked him "to ordain a pious man" for service in America. Lowth's reply was a bare negative. Then the resourceful and independent Wesley resolved to act on a conclusion he had reached forty years before. In 1746, he had read a book by Lord King, which had been published in 1691. After reading it, he wrote in his *Journal:* "In spite of the vehement prejudice of my education, I was ready to believe that this was a fair and impartial draught. But if so, it would follow that bishops and presbyters are (essentially) of one order, and that originally every Christian congregation was a church independent of all others." This "fair and impartial draught" was a book by Lord King entitled *An Enquiry into the Constitution, Discipline, Unity and Worship of the Primitive Church, that Flourish'd within the First Three Hundred Years after Christ. Faithfully Collected out of the Extant Writings of those Ages. By an Impartial Hand.* This Lord King (Peter King) was a man of parts—member of Parliament, lawyer, chief justice of the common pleas court, speaker of the House of Lords, and finally lord chancellor. His commonsense acceptance of fact as over against hierarchical pretensions was seen not only in this book that he wrote but also in the fact that he was the author of the Act of virtue by which English superseded Latin as the language of the courts.

His book is the most scholarly piece of research on this subject with which I am acquainted. I have read a yellowed copy, printed in the old style of type and letters, which was printed in London "for F. Wyat at the Rose, and R. Robinson at the Golden-Lyon, in St. Paul's Church-Yard. 1713."

At the risk of repeating what I have said above, let me give a brief summary of Lord King's findings. He shows that each congregation was presided over by a bishop (that is, by an *episkopos,* or overseer, or chairman presbyter, or presiding elder—they all mean the same thing). Each bishop had one or more assistants of the same order, called elders or presbyters. There were also deacons who served the tables and cared for the poor, and did work of that kind. The deacons were part of the governing body of the church, participating in matters of discipline, in the calling and deposing of bishops and elders and such work.

No one bishop was superior to another. The idea that the bishop of the congregation at Rome was superior to the bishop at Carthage, or Antioch, or Jerusalem, or Alexandria, or any other place, cannot be substantiated by any historical evidence of the first three hundred years of the Christian era. When a synod convened, the synod chose the bishop who was to preside. Victor, the Bishop of Rome, was prolocutor of a synod held there; Palamas, Bishop of Amastris, was Moderator of a synod held in Pontus; Irenaeus, Bishop of Lyons, was Moderator of a synod held in France. Polycrates, Bishop of Ephesus, presided over a synod of African bishops. A convocation in Palestine had two moderators, namely: Theophilus, Bishop of Caesarea, and Narcissus, Bishop of Jerusalem.

John Wesley's powerful and discriminating application of logic and history to the questions of orders demolished all unwarranted assumptions and papal pretensions. His decision to ordain men for the administering of the Sacraments to his followers in America was born of historic fact and reflection rather than of prejudice and impulse. Thirty-eight years before he ordained anybody, that is, in 1746, he said, after reading Lord King's book, "I was *ready* to believe that this was a fair and impartial draught. . . . Bishops and presbyters are (essentially) of one order." This makes it clear that what Wesley did in 1784 was not done impulsively, but deliberately—a course of action determined upon as a result of careful thought. It was this: When the Church of England Bishop of London refused to ordain a man whom Wesley might send to America, Wesley decided to ordain as Superintendent, Thomas Coke, a graduate of Oxford University with a doctor's degree, a scholarly Anglican clergyman who seven years earlier had thrown in his lot with the Methodists. The ordination took place in Bristol on the 2nd of September, 1784. James Creighton, an ordained minister of the Church of England, joined with Wesley in setting apart Coke as Superintendent. The same day, John Wesley and Thomas Coke and James Creighton, as Presbyters, laid hands on Richard Whatcoat and Thomas Vasey, and ordained them elders in the Church of God, to be sent with Coke to America. Wesley later ordained other men for work in Scotland, Canada, and England.

Dr. Coke met with Francis Asbury and other Methodist preachers (American and those sent by Wesley) in the famous Christmas Conference of 1784, held in Baltimore, at which time and place they organized the Methodist Episcopal Church. Asbury would not permit Coke to ordain him unless and until the Methodist preachers, in Conference assembled, should elect him for ordination and leadership. This they did unanimously. Then Coke, assisted by both Whatcoat and Vasey and also by Philip William Otterbein, a pietistic German Reformed minister, ordained Asbury, first as deacon, then as elder, and then set him apart as superintendent. The Conference also elected Coke as a superintendent.

The Methodist Church steadfastly holds to the ordination of deacons and elders for the conferring of holy orders, and for consecration of duly elected elders to the office of bishop. Although Coke and Asbury were elected as superintendents, they were at once called Bishops. Whether they consciously passed from superintendent or overseer to *episkopos* or bishop, I do not know; but I do know that from the beginning of the Methodist Church in America, our chief officers have been called bishops. In Methodism, however, the episcopacy is not an order conferred by ordination, but an office and work into which a chosen elder is inducted by a solemn and dignified ritual of consecration.

We believe in the apostolic succession of the ministry, unbroken from apostolic days to the present. We believe in the apostolic succession of Christian fellowship, called the Christian Church. We believe in the apostolic succession of Christian consecration and zeal. We also believe that we are great not because we are heirs of a great past, but only in proportion as we possess the passion that made the past great. In the words of the Report which "The Joint Commission on Approaches to Unity," submitted to the General Convention of the Protestant Episcopal Church in 1949, we hold that "the fundamental Christian ministry is the ministry of Christ.

84

There is no Christian priesthood or ministry apart from His. His priestly and ministerial function is to reconcile the world to God in and through Himself, by His Incarnation and by His 'one sacrifice once offered' and by the gift of the Holy Spirit, delivering men from the power of sin and death.

"The Church as the Body of Christ, sharing His life, has a ministerial function derived from that of Christ. In this function every member has his place and share according to his different capabilities and calling. The Church is set before us in the New Testament as a body of believers having within it, as its recognized focus of unity, of teaching and of authority, the Apostolate, which owed its origin to the action of the Lord Himself. There was not first an Apostolate which gathered a body of believers about itself; nor was there a completely structureless collection of believers which gave authority to the Apostles to speak and act on its behalf. From the first there was the fellowship of believers finding its unity in the Twelve. Thus the New Testament bears witness to the principle of a distinctive ministry, as an original element, but not the sole constitutive element in the life of the Church."

We further hold that "the maintenance of a ministerial succession, by way of ordination with the laying on of hands, is a familiar fact in the life of most Christian communions. All such ministerial successions are in some sense historic, differing from one another, however, in form and in the degree to which succession is continuous in history."

85

CHAPTER VII

Sacraments in the Life of the Church

By CHARLES D. KEAN

Sacraments are operative only within the life of the Holy People of God. They have their roots not only in the historic origins of the Christian movement, but also in its ongoing and unfolding life. They are means by which the fellowship of those who respond in faith to the saving work of Christ is related dynamically to His transforming power and sustaining strength.

The Church makes possible the sacraments, but on the other hand sacraments in principle make it possible for the Church to be the Church: a living fellowship with historical continuity and immediate relevance, in and through which the wall of partition between man and God and man and man is breached. They both relate the Holy Catholic Church of faith to the changing scene of human striving, and in the reverse direction they make it possible for the immediate local and historical organizations of Christian people to transcend their limitations of vision, understanding, perspective and historical situation so as to be able to be part of the saving work of God in the world.

All religious groups, whether or not they use the word, *sacrament,* have symbolic rites which use immediate and at least quasi-material things to be the bearers of what, in the last analysis, remains an indefinable reality. The first part of the phrase in the Anglican catechism—"I mean by this word, sacrament, an outward and visible sign of an inward and spiritual grace," is applicable by analogy to the religious experience in most peoples in the world, since all men must make their faith, whatever it is, concrete and also find some kind of transcendant significance for their struggles in historical situations. Without some such means religion cannot function.

Sacraments are means by which the faith of the fellowship, whether Christian or not, makes vital contact with the life situations of the members, both in the general sense of hallowing human nature and in the more specific sense of sanctifying the particular experiences of particular people. Thus the Christian tradition knows of sacraments in the setting of a broad spectrum, brightest in connection with the two great sacraments common to all Christian people—Baptism and the Holy Communion—and ranging out through the five minor sacraments of Western Catholic tradition, to a great number of quasi-sacramental acts and services for hallowing the common life.

Sacraments, then, are of the essence of living religion. But in every case sacraments presuppose the existence of a fellowship of shared faith which uses its ordinances in the light of its convictions and commitments. Without sacramental instrumentalities of some kind, religion is sterilized—it becomes simply philosophy and ethics, an externalized, intellectual enterprise without vitality. On the other hand, except within the fellowship of faith (and in many non-Christian settings even within such a fellowship) sacraments degenerate into magic—which means that individuals and groups are trying to manipulate the universe to serve their own ends.

Returning to the phrase in the Anglican catechism, the strictly Christian note is given by the rest of the definition, describing what kind of sacramental rites interest Christian people. "Given unto us, ordained by Christ himself, as a means whereby we receive this grace and a pledge to assure us thereof." In other words, the specifically Christian note about sacraments—that which defines Christian sacraments as such in contradistinction to other symbolic uses of material things to be bearers of a transcendent significance for the users—is in the understanding, "given unto us, ordained by Christ himself."

Such an understanding cannot be accepted simply on the verbal level. In order that its meaning be clear, it is necessary to think of it in the context of the relationship of Christ to the Church which uses the phrase. We are not simply concerned with ancient origins, but with continuing transforming power and sustaining strength.

The use of sacraments, in the Christian sense, depends upon the prior conviction that Christ is Lord of the Church today, that He works through His Church here and now, and that men and women in and through the Church are drawn close to Him. He is not simply present in mysterious form in religious services but also in the daily experience of Christian people. Without such a conviction underlying the discussion of sacraments, there is no point whatsoever to studying the subject.

The Sacraments are "given unto us" not simply in the fact that they can be traced back to primitive beginnings in Apostolic times. Indeed, scholars have legitimate differences of opinion as to the precise way or ways in which the original apostolic band and its immediate successors began to use those ordinances which have marked the main stream of Christianity ever since. We do not need to debate here how the Eucharist evolved from the Jewish Kiddush and Kibburah meals, or how Holy Baptism was adapted from Old Testament ritual washings via the intermediate stage of John the Baptist. The scholars can work with these problems and we can learn from what they find.

What does concern us today, just as much as it concerned the first century Christian Church is that the worship life of our fellowship provides an accurate and adequate basis for the dynamic encounter of our Living Lord with men and women who are involved in the actual struggles of daily living. The Christian Church asserts that the sacraments of Holy Baptism and the Holy Communion are given unto us in this sense. They are completely congruent with both the original apostolic experience and the Church's continuing understanding of what kind of a Lord we acknowledge.

"Ordained by Christ himself, as a means whereby we receive this grace." The cornerstone of the life of the Christian fellowship is the shared conviction of those who have any legitimate claim to be called Christians that "by grace are we saved through faith." The Christian religion is the identification of living men and women with a fellowship which dares to believe that through its commitment, individually and corporately, to the Living Lord the perennial autonomous tendencies in every human being can be

88

overcome. This victory we claim as ours, not by our achievements nor our merits, but by trusting in God as we know Him revealed in Jesus Christ.

The continual tendency of every individual person and every organized human group is to usurp the role of God in history. The Christian faith knows this tendency to be overcome only through the Cross, and this redemption enters the stream of human affairs through the acceptance of the Cross by faith in the hearts of individual men and women and is reflected in their individual and group life. The Christian Church from the very beginning has asserted that its sacraments are means whereby the saving Grace of God appropriated by faith becomes effective in the lives of men and women in the actual world.

When we discuss the meaning of sacraments in the context of serious concern about the life of the Christian Church and our part in it, everything we think and say is conditioned by the Christian Faith. Any tradition within history tends to attract to itself varying and tangential accretions in the form of interpretation and practice, and these often confuse the underlying issue. Our concern is with the Sacraments as instrumentalities for the life of faith in the fellowship of Christian people. That which is not clearly connected with this concern is irrelevant, no matter how ancient it may be. That which clarifies the concern is significant. We are first of all Christians and only secondly theorists.

When we consider the faith of the Church in some genuinely practical context, we must be concerned with the sacramental instrumentalities by which it is related to real people facing real problems in a real world. Likewise when we consider the human situation with complete realism and on guard against illusions as to the natural goodness of human nature, the necessity for a sacramental channel for the practical acceptance and appreciation of the Christian point of view is obvious. Man is neither pure mind nor free spirit as he is encountered within history.

I. *Holy Baptism*

Holy Baptism has been the traditional initiation rite of the Christian fellowship since the beginning. It is the incorporation of

89

the individual into the Body of Christ. The development of sects practicing "believers' baptism" reinforces such an understanding rather than the reverse. The real difference between them and the groups practicing infant baptism as the normal thing is not in the age at which persons are initiated, nor even in the supposed maturity of the initiates, nor even in divergent theories about the rite itself, but rather in the understanding of the nature of the Church.

Holy Baptism is a sacrament which defines the relationship of the indvidual to the fellowship. Therefore, in a fundamental sense, it provides the basis for all other sacraments and sacramental rites because these presuppose some kind of relationship already to exist. Therefore, the primary issue in considering Holy Baptism is: what kind of a relationship between man and God does the Church provide?

It is not within the province of this paper to deal with the background in Jewish thought and practice, nor with primitive Christian practice and understanding as such. (Cullman's work is very illuminating here.) This study is concerned with the kind of relationship between man and God in the context of the Christian fellowship which Holy Baptism dramatizes and explains.

The Christian Church is a fellowship of men and women who are "one in Christ Jesus," through their acceptance in faith of the saving work of God in Christ. This fellowship is God's achievement in the primary sense. It is the result of the divine initiative acting in history. Yet the outward form and the administration of the day-by-day life of the fellowship, its organization and details of practice, are the result of man's response (admittedly qualified and incomplete) to God's demand.

The role of the fellowship within history is to be the loyal people of God, "the Holy Nation" of I Peter. It is consequently its duty to reach out as widely as possible to include all those whom it can reach within the Holy Nation. But such an enterprise is the concommitant of faith, and can only be considered in the light of Christian faith. Therefore, the inclusion of new members within the fellowship must be in terms of the faith by which the fellowship itself lives, else the inclusion process will itself destroy the fellowship.

Again, we repeat that the fellowship itself exists in the shared awareness of those who comprise it that "while we were yet sinners Christ died for us." Its processes of extension rests upon the premise that the "we" referred to in the passage from the Epistle to the Romans applies to all who respond in faith to God's initiative. Yet, not even the response is man's good work. Justification and sanctification are not built upon our having the right attitude or the correct emotional feelings any more than they depend upon some external and mechanical operation. Yet, on the other hand, the response is real—so real that Christian experience uses the words "death" and "new birth" to describe what happens.

The response of faith to the divine initiative is the act of the whole Church. It is in this sense that the fellowship can be called the Body of Christ. Jesus Christ, as the Christian faith knows him, alone of all men responded completely to the divine demand. The Church is the fellowship of those who are identified with his response by faith and whose trust, therefore, is not in the perfectability of human beings by themselves, but in the encounter with the Father and the Son, in the communion of the Holy Spirit.

This understanding is what underlies the Sacrament of Holy Baptism, and it is particularly made clear by the ancient practice of infant baptism. The infant can claim no credit whatsoever for being baptized. The fellowship dares to include him within its membership, as a citizen of the Holy Nation, not because of anything he has said or done or understood, but because he can, through the Grace of God, be a sharer in the promise, "While we were yet sinners, Christ died for us."

The Christian Church, as the Body of Christ, reaches out and claims the child. Yet this is not an automatic thing. The parents and sponsors promise to see that the child grows up instructed in doctrine and conduct. The fellowship, at the very outset, as in the Anglican form—"Wilt thou take heed that this Child, so soon as sufficiently instructed, be brought to the Bishop to be confirmed by Him"—states that the infant initiate will be called upon

91

consciously to take upon himself the commitments made for him. But the child will grow up within the fellowship. He will never know himself apart from the Scriptural promise. He will never know his own existence apart from the background of the brotherhood. The Church will provide the frame of reference for his gropings and strivings.

The service of Holy Baptism is the denial made by Christian faith to the blind optimism of nineteenth and twentieth century naturalism. Certainly the structure of society will change from age to age. The details of our problems differ from those which our ancestors faced, and also from those with which our grandchildren will have to deal. But every child who has ever been born in this world, and who ever will be born until the end of time, is made in "the image of God" and is consequently capable of—not only capable but likely to—turning this creation into a usurpation. The man will never be born who will not need the transforming power and sustaining strength of the Cross to save him from pretending to be God and to save his brothers from the tragic results of such pretension.

The Sacrament of Holy Baptism, is, therefore, a frank recognition of both the assets and liabilities of human nature. It is an acceptance of life's demand in terms of the way life really works. It constitutes a transference of the death of Christ to individual people, because it is only as man shares the Cross by faith that he can die to himself and be re-born as a free member of the fellowship. If he does not die to his own egotism, he will use his God-given capabilities destructively without knowing his own need for redemption. If he is identified by faith with the fellowship, his sins and victories are both within the framework of the divine forgiveness over-ruling man's egotistic tendencies.

Holy Baptism says that the Church is the fellowship of those who know their own need, who know themselves to be sinners, and who know themselves apart from Christ to be hopelessly involved in "the body of this death." It is not the association of the virtuous nor of the wise who use some symbolic rite to emphasize the high estate to which they have climbed. Rather the Church is the brotherhood of ordinary garden variety men and women who trust God and dare in faith to think of themselves as members of the Body of Christ. Since man by his own accomplishments can never find the Cross unnecessary, the Church shows this to be so by initiating into its fellowship those who have no accomplishments at all.

Finally, Holy Baptism says something about the Christian family and the Church. The family brings the child to be baptized. The family accepts its responsibilities—which would be its anyhow—in the framework of the larger fellowship. Thus by the rite of Baptism the family becomes *Ecclesiola in Ecclesia*—the little Church within the Church; and in reverse the Church shows that the pattern of the human family at its best is the highest historical manifestation of the divine pattern for society.

II. *The Holy Communion*

The Holy Communion from the very earliest days of the Christian Church has been the central rite of its ongoing life. In this sense, it can be said that the Holy Communion is the distinctively Christian note in the worship of the Church, so that all other acts and forms of worship are to be understood in its light. At the service of the Holy Communion, the fellowship is distinctively conscious of being the body of Christ; and at the service of Holy Communion, the Christian Church is known to be the connecting link between the Living Lord and the details of the daily lives of those who claim identification with Him. Without the Holy Communion in some such sense as this the Christian Church is an abstraction—it does not really exist within history.

As Holy Baptism defines dramatically the relationship of the individual to God and to his fellowman in and through the life of the Church, so the Holy Communion defines dramatically the continuing life of the fellowship in its role as the living context within which men and women are related to God and to each other "in Christ." The Church, so defined, is first of all, therefore, to be understood in the light of the Christian faith, and all other aspects of its organized, historical continuity are to be interpreted in this context.

The Epistle to the Galatians says, "As many as have been baptized have put on Christ, where there is neither Greek nor Jew, where there is neither bond nor free, where there is neither male nor female, for ye are all one in Christ Jesus." The Holy Communion is the sacramental act by which the Church in the course of its ongoing history re-affirms this understanding and at the same time re-affirms its own need to understand its own life this way.

The dichotomy of the individual and society is the raw material of historical tragedy, because the individual is always prone to assert his own selfhood against society regardless of the objective meaning of circumstance, while society is always tempted to suppress the individuality of men and women, subjecting them to an authoritarian group. In contradistinction to this dichotomy the Christian Church sets forth a relationship in which the individual and society are each free to fulfill their distinctive roles in history in fruitful, as against destructive, tension with each other.

We are "one in Christ Jesus" not because our individuality has been suppressed, but because the Cross has become the decisive, the determinative, factor in our experience. But the fellowship is equally real since it overcomes the divisions between Greek and Jew, bond and free, male and female. Free men in a free fellowship is the Christian Church's understanding of its own life.

But such a life is only possible in faith. It is not historically demonstrable. The members of the Church in actuality are related to it ambiguously—both as loyally participating and as still claiming autonomy. The organized social structure likewise is ambiguous—at one and the same time judging itself by and trying to conform itself to the Christ whose Body it bears, and arrogating to itself on the human and historical level a "divine" sanction for dictation over the minds and bodies of living people. Within history, the Church contains much that contradicts itself even as it bears witness to the faith.

The Sacrament of the Holy Communion, therefore, serves the purpose of relating the Church to its Lord—who is Lord both over the individual lives of the members and over the corporate life of the group. And the relationship is in terms of the Christian faith itself—"while we were yet sinners Christ died for us," so that by identification with Him, in spite of our individual and social

94

sin we are still "one in Christ Jesus." Every celebration of the Holy Communion is the re-statement of the fact that "by grace are we saved through faith, and that not of ourselves; it is the gift of God."

"In the Supper of the Lord the faithful receive and partake, spiritually, of the Body and Blood of Christ; and thus enter into communion with Christ Himself and with one another in His Life." (Faith and Order Statement of 1949.)

The purpose of the sacrament of the Holy Communion is to make available the transforming and sustaining power of the Living Lord to his Church—both to make possible the continuing response in faith, and also to relate the faith itself to history. If the divisions which separate men as individuals from each other, and as warring groups within society, are only overcome in principle at the altar rail (and not in daily practice) then the life of the Church is the most tragic of tragedies.

Every service of the Holy Communion is, therefore, our individual and group re-identification with the Cross and Resurrection of Christ, by faith in which alone we are able to say that we are "one in Christ Jesus." Every celebration of the Sacrament is then a sanctification of our common life with all its complications and involvements, because it is in our common life of home and business, of community and world, that our autonomous tendencies wreak havoc. Every communication by the faithful believer is the infusing of the spirit of Christ into the organized life of the world.

The service of the Holy Communion dramatizes the fact that in God's Province "the kingdoms of this world are become the Kingdom of our God and of His Christ." But this does not take place by the superimposition of the Church upon the political and economic order as if it were a higher legal authority. It takes place as "the colony of heaven"—the *politeuma* of the Epistle to the Philippians—accepts its own role in history with penitence and faith.

The Holy Communion also involves sacrifice. As the *Book of Common Prayer* puts it—"And here we offer unto thee, O Lord, our selves, our souls and bodies, to be a reasonable, holy and living sacrifice unto thee, humbly beseeching thee that we and all others who shall be partakers of this Holy Communion, may worthily receive the most precious Body and Blood of thy Son Jesus Christ, be filled with thy grace and heavenly benediction, and made one body with him, that he may dwell in us, and we in him. And although we are unworthy, through our manifold sins, to offer unto thee any sacrifice; yet we beseech thee to accept this our bounden duty and service; not weighing our merits, but pardoning our offences, through Jesus Christ our Lord. . ."

The offering of the Holy Communion is the offering of the whole fellowship as the Church, responds in faith to God whose offering of himself in Christ brings the Church into being. And as long as history, with its tensions and cross-currents, continues to be what we know it to be, the faith of the fellowship must be continually re-focussed on the Cross again and again and again, in order that the Church may serve as the "colony of heaven." Through the Holy Communion, the individual worshipper re-affirms his solidarity with the "Holy Nation" as understood in Christian faith, and the Church re-affirms its own mission.

"The Lord's Supper shows forth the Lord's death till He come. It is offered as the memorial of His sacrifice which He commanded us to make in which the faithful also offer themselves as a living sacrifice to God through him." (Faith and Order Statement, 1949.)

The Sacrament is the distinctively Christian means through which God draws man—in his Church-consciousness—close to Himself in order that the Word of God may be spoken to the world through the daily life of the Church member. The sacrament is the means whereby men and women who are always ambiguously related to concrete historical issues again and again are enabled to appreciate the centrality of the faith for the issues which concern them.

Just as the human body must continually receive new proteins, carbohydrates, vitamins and minerals along with water if it is to continue to live, the Christian individual and the Christian group need the continual replenishing of faith through deliberate contact with the Lord of the Church. Otherwise the way of the world takes over. But the objective operation viewed merely for itself may actually mean that the way of the world is taking over under the guise of a Christian sacrament. While a duly authorized ministry is necessary, it must be remembered that our ultimate dependence is on the Grace of God.

III. *The Operation of the Sacraments*

There have been many times in Christian history when men have tried to analyze the process by which the Sacraments were efficacious in a way analogous to feeding people radio-active elements in their food so as to follow the digestive process. But sacraments are authenticated in the ongoing life of the fellowship, as the fellowship understands its own existence in terms of Christian faith.

No discussion of the meaning of sacraments can ever get far from these premises without compromising the essentially Christian note. The twin dangers in any consideration of sacraments are, on the one hand, "mechanical" theories, and, on the other hand, "receptionist" theories. The former externalizes the issue—making sacramental meaning a derivative of organizational structure, the qualifications of the officiant, or the actual things used and done. The latter cuts the connection between individual existence and history so as to make religion a matter of feelings and reactions.

A New Testament understanding of the Church as "The Holy Nation" makes it possible to avoid both dangers. Since the fellowship itself is broken in its organized life today, it is not surprising that there is confusion about the Sacraments. In order to have the administration of the ordinances at all, it is necessary that there be some kind of ecclesiastical structure, authorization of ministers, and accepted understanding of proper ways and means. But it is one thing to recognize that in a divided Church, there will be resulting divisions in the ways of administering and interpreting sacramental process, and quite another thing to say that any particular variation alone has divine sanctions.

One of the difficulties in considering any serious religious issue today is that every observer tends to read the situation he knows today back into Church history, and to understand the origins of

Christian traditions in the light of his own experience. While this is only natural, as all historians realized it is also tragic. Denominationalism as we know it is more the outgrowth of the settlement of 1688 in England, and the conditions of the American frontier between 1750 and 1890, than it is a matter of differing views on sacraments and order. Before 1688, the questions which disturb the ecumenical movements today did not seem to bother the various Reformed Churches of Europe—and not at least in the same way that they perplex us.

When the meaning and operation of sacraments is looked at primarily in terms of the life of the fellowship, the whole problem appears different from the way we usually see it. The fellowship has two poles of reference exercising together a fruitful tension on its life and actions. The first pole is, of course, the life, work, teaching, Cross and Resurrection of Jesus Christ, and the experience of the Apostolic Church. The other pole is man's practical encounter with the problems which confront him today. We avoid fruitless digressions into mechanics and sensations when we approach sacraments from this point of view.

An illustration of the application of the principle is to be found in what happened to the custom of the *Agape,* which certainly had sacramental significance in the life of the early Church, but which disappeared from the normal life of the Church before the era of systematizing liturgical theology. There is every reason to believe that the *Agape* had a significance only exceeded by Holy Baptism and the Holy Communion in the practice, if not in the stated theory, of the Church of the second century, and it certainly held a greater place than other sacramental rites. In the post-Nicaean Church, however, the *Agape* lost contact with the pole of immediate relevance, and despite its acknowledged New Testament background (carried back to the stories of the miraculous feedings in the Gospels), it disappeared from Christian practice.

In a contrary way, Holy Matrimony which certainly was not a sacrament in the life and practice of the primitive Christian community has come to have a very great significance in the modern world where the survival of the family is one of the great crisis questions of our day. As the relationship of the Church to common life became generally accepted, marriage became part of the Church's responsibility, but only the most far-fetched New Testament exegesis can find any connection between the Johannine story of the Marriage at Cana and the problem the fellowship actually faces in real life. This is not to say that there is no legitimate connection between Holy Matrimony and the New Testament.

It is the fellowship with its faith in the saving power of Christ that continues essentially the same, rather than the details of its liturgical practice. The two great Sacraments, Holy Baptism and the Holy Communion, are so basically related to what is perennially true about man in history that their central meaning and acts continue the same through the millenia of Christian history. But even these have seen great changes in detailed practice, growing out of the changing needs of men in a changing world.

Liturgical scholars like to show the points of similarity between the Anglican Eucharist of the 20th century and the Apostolic Constitutions of the 3rd (4th) century. It might be even more illuminating to point to the differences in form and custom in such a way as to show that the central act of faith is the same despite them.

In the Sacraments, the fellowship dramatizes dynamically its own unqualified dependence upon the grace of God in Christ Jesus. If this central sense of dependence is absent, or even played down, there is a deficiency in sacramental practice despite every possible test of regularity as to the authority of the ministers, the precise use of words and acts, and the unchallenged antiquity of the rite.

In the Sacraments, the fellowship takes seriously its role as the Holy Nation, the *politeuma,* the colony of heaven in an unredeemed world. This is not a question of feelings or opinions. It is primarily a question of concerned men and women, welded through shared faith in brotherhood with each other, finding in its central traditional rites of worship a dynamic way of bringing to focus the love and power of God, in Christ Jesus, upon the problems which the world faces. The living fellowship is that which is concerned to bring the redeeming power of God—not just a Christian ethic—to bear upon the great contemporary issues of world peace, general economic prosperity, the role of the family in an ur-

99

ban society, the freedom of the individual man in a technological era. The sacramental practices of any group of people must sharpen the cutting edge of both the individual lives of the members and the group as a whole for dealing with the real problems of the real world.

When these two essential premises are the common understanding of any negotiating churches, then there is a basis upon which differences may be faced. In this context, questions of order and validity can be dealt with. But aside from this context, these questions have no intelligible meaning for those who take the Christian faith seriously.

CHAPTER VIII

The Sacraments in The Methodist Church

By RUFUS C. BAKER

American Methodism received its Liturgy in 1784 from the hand of Rev. John Wesley, a loyal priest in the Anglican Church. This Liturgy was entitled: "The Sunday service of Methodists in North America, with Other Occasional Services." In his letter of transmissal, Wesley said, "I believe there is no Liturgy in the world, either in ancient or modern language, which breathes more of a solid, scriptural, rational Piety, than the Common Prayer of the Church of England." In his "Sunday Service," Wesley took a great many liberties with the *Book of Common Prayer* in adapting it for Methodists. He omitted many of the holy days; he shortened the service for the Lord's Day; he omitted certain imprecatory Psalms.

Wesley followed the ritual of the Anglican Communion fairly closely. He made certain changes in the rubrics; for example he substituted "elder" for "priest." He omitted some of the sentences in the offices of Baptism and Burial of the Dead. He included no ritual for the private Baptism of infants. In the Communion ritual, the recital of the Nicene Creed and the Exhortations that precede the Invitation in the *Book of Common Prayer* were omitted. It can be said, however, that in essence both the Communion Ritual and that for the office of Baptism are the same as in the *Book of Common Prayer*. In his communication accompanying the Liturgy, Wesley placed strong emphasis on the Sacraments, urging a weekly observance of the Lord's Supper.

Wesley's conception of the function of the Sacraments was grounded in his doctrinal views; especially as they related to the fall, Adamic guilt or original sin and the plan of redemption as wrought out in Jesus Christ. Wesley's interpretation of the function of Baptism is stated thus by Dr. Webb B. Garrison: "John Wesley's position concerning the doctrine of original sin is basic in any consideration of his view of baptism. Long passages in his sermons and letters are pervaded by an unmistakable conviction that the 'natural man' is utterly depraved. . . . Man is incapable of doing anything to rid himself of that (Adamic) guilt. He can only accept God's grace, which is freely bestowed but never earned. But, said Wesley, 'God's grace must have a channel through which to operate! That channel he declared to be baptism, the sacrament being but an outward symbol of an inward cleansing. For him the rite was far from a mere dedication. It involved certain benefits inevitably conferred by baptism, and available in no other way." Concerning Holy Communion Dr. Garrison says: "His (Wesley's) view of the Lord's Supper made it the agency of cleansing for post-baptismal sins." Then Dr. Garrison points out how succeeding General Conferences have revised and modified the sacramental rites which Wesley included in the first Methodist service book, and I quote: "Succeeding sessions of the General Conference have removed every reference to original sin, the devil and the wrath of God. There have been verbal changes in each passage based on the doctrine that man inherits a fallen nature. . . . For Wesley's doctrine that the natural man is at enmity with God, . . . the present baptismal forms convey the contrary assurance that 'all men are heirs of life eternal and subjects of the saving grace of the Holy Spirit.' . . . There remains in the text not an illusion to the work of the Sacrament (Baptism) as a cleansing agent."

Dr. Garrison calls our attention to the further fact that the Communion Ritual in the longer form contains no reference to the elements as a means of cleansing the communicant of sin, expressing only the hope that in partaking of the communion the communicant "may be filled with the fullness of his (Jesus Christ's) life, may grow into his likeness, and may evermore dwell in him and he in us." It also may be observed that in the prayer of consecration in this longer form we have changed the phrase, "may be partakers of his blessed body and blood" to read "may also be partakers of the divine nature through him. . . ." It should be noted, however, that in the Shorter Form the Ritual remains substantially as given to us in Wesley's Order of Worship, which would indicate that Methodists are not unanimous in their theological concepts nor disposed to be dogmatic in the matter of the Form to be used.

Until recent years American Methodism has made evangelism and a ministry to the people on the expanding frontier its primary concern. Methodist missionaries and evangelists held religious services in homes, halls, brush arbors, tents, school houses and simple, and sometimes crude, chapels provided by the hardy pioneers. While the Sacraments were faithfully observed, the situation did not lend itself to liturgical services. The emphasis was laid on salvation by faith. Repentance was a prerequisite and ethical living the fruitage. Preaching was and continues to be central in Methodist religious worship. Actually, Wesley's Sunday Service was unpopular with American Methodists, and apparently fell into disuse by 1800.

But with the passing of the old frontier a new development in Methodist interest and practice is clearly in evidence. There is a very definite trend toward Gothic architecture, with its altar and divided chancel, and the use of a more elaborate liturgy in worship. As early as 1932 the former Methodist Episcopal Church restored to the Communion Ritual much of the material that was in the "Sunday Service" prepared by Wesley and this fuller form was incorporated in the ritual of The Methodist Church by the Uniting Conference of 1939. This interest in an enriched liturgy was further evidenced by the authorization of the publication of *"The Book of Worship* for voluntary and optional use" by the General Conference of 1944.

Methodists recognize many means of grace, but only two Sacraments. With the Free Church theologians of Great Britain, Methodists "hold that Baptism and Holy Communion are the Sacraments of the Gospel, of divine ordinance, necessary to the Church and of perpetual obligation. By the first we are incorporated into the Church, by the second we are sanctified in the Church." Methodists would agree with them when they say further that "the Sacraments are signs and seals of the Gospel of Christ, and, through the power of the Holy Spirit, means of grace where-

103

by Christ is present in the divinely appointed ordinances." It is in this that the sacramental nature of the rites inhere. The Sacraments are not "mere forms." They are divinely appointed means of grace and occupy a distinctive place in Methodist thought and practice. Dr. Oscar Thomas Olson correctly says, "Methodism has endeavored to shift the center of gravity from authority to experience by magnifying the sacramental principle of faith rather than the rites and ceremonies of the Sacraments." But this does not mean any lack of appreciation of the value of the rites and ceremonies as aids to faith and means of grace.

By the same token, Methodists see no magical efficacy in the Sacraments. Their benefits do not derive from the administration and partaking of the Sacraments, per se. For those of riper years, their benefits are conditioned by and dependent upon the attitude of the soul. For infants, the benefits derive from the faith of parents or sponsors and the Church, and the act of incorporation into the Church. The efficacy in every case is in the act rather than the elements. An act in which God, the Church and the participants share. The material elements of water, bread and wine are merely divinely appointed means by which the living Lord becomes in every truth "Emmanuel, God with us."

Bishop Frank Westcott in his *Catholic Principles* says: "If the question be asked how and in what way the Lord is present in the Sacraments, our reply must always be that the Church as a whole refuses to define the nature of the Lord's presence. . . . She believes and teaches the *fact* of his presence, without professing to understand the *mode* of that presence. She affirms that it is *objective* and not a *subjective consciousness;* that it is *mystical* and *spiritual* and not *material,* and beyond this she cannot go." Methodists would subscribe to this statement, and beyond this Methodists could not go.

We would agree with Canon Theodore O. Wedel when he says, "Sacraments are of the essence of corporate historical existence." They partake of and give expression to the principle of universality in the Body of Christ. They afford an historical and valid basis for ecumenicity, and in the observance of them we declare our oneness with all Christendom.

104

As already suggested, Baptism is the divinely ordained rite of entrance into the "New Israel," the Messianic Community, the people of God, drawn from every nation, tribe, race and language. In this sense it can be said to be the door of the Church, the Body of Christ. The primary significance of the rite is that of certifying one for entrance into the Fellowship. In their approach to Baptism, "Catholic" bodies have stressed the sacramental point of view. Many "Protestants" have insisted upon a purely symbolic interpretation. Dr. Clarence Tucker Craig is correct when he says, "Sacrament and symbol need to be held together. . . . A complete view of Baptism will hold together symbol and sacrament, and dissolve neither in the other."

Methodists believe in and practice infant baptism, not as a *sine qua non* of infant salvation, but as a means of parental dedication and consecration of the child to God and his Church, and an induction of the child, who with all men is an heir of life eternal and a subject of the saving grace of the Holy Spirit, into the Church. The work of salvation is not thereby finished. It is only begun. Parents or sponsors must agree to see that the child is trained to give reverent attendance upon private and public worship of God and the teaching of the Holy Scriptures; and in every way by precept and example seek to lead him into the love of God and the service of our Lord Jesus Christ. And pastors are enjoined to gather baptized children into Preparatory Membership classes when they have reached the age of twelve years, or at an earlier age when it is deemed advisable, to instruct them in the nature, design and obligations of Baptism, and in the truths of the Scriptures; after which they must make a public declaration of their personal faith in God, their acceptance of Christ as their personal Savior, and be formally confirmed by the laying on of hands and the use of a ritualistic formula very similar to the one in use in the Anglican Communion.

In dealing specifically with the sacrament of the Lord's Supper, this additional word should be said. Dr. Olson says, "The definitive idea of the Holy Communion was the commemoration of a sacrifice." It is not a repetition of that sacrifice. Methodists hold that Christ made on the Cross "by the offering of himself, a

105

full, perfect and sufficient sacrifice for the sins of the whole world." Therefore, "The Priest," as Dr. Clarence Tucker Craig has so well said, "cannot offer up Christ again and again if his sacrifice was really once and for all." We can and do "offer and present . . . ourselves, our souls and bodies, to be a reasonable, holy and living sacrifice" in the act of Holy Communion, but not a fresh offering up of Christ.

The Methodist Church is not a "confessional" church. It, therefore, requires no recital of a creed as a pre-requisite to Communion. It uses the Ten Commandments, the Beatitudes and selected portions of the Book of Isaiah in its Communion Ritual, but no creed. Earnest repentance, love and charity and an intention to lead a new life following the commandments of God, are all the Methodist Church requires of those who would come to the Lord's table.

John Wesley was sure the Lord's Supper could be a "converting ordinance." But Methodist tradition and usage has shifted the emphasis elsewhere. It is a means of sanctifying grace. As Dr. Umphrey Lee has said, "The sacrament (Communion) is a memorial, a sign of present grace, a means of grace, a pledge of future glory, a commemorative service, a sacrifice of ourselves and our goods." Dr. Olson puts it this way: "The Sacrament of the Lord's Supper has a three-fold meaning for American Methodists. First: It is a feast of memory . . . Second: It is a festival of the living Christ, as he promised to be with those who meet in his name, remembering his cross . . . Third: it is a prophecy of the victory of God." In Communion it is truly the *Lord's* Supper. He is the host. We sit at the table and in spirit feed on him in our hearts by faith, with thanksgiving.

CHAPTER IX

Baptism and Church Unity

By ALEXANDER C. ZABRISKIE

1. This paper was presented to a group of Methodists and Episcopalians. Responsibility for its contents is mine alone, but the original draft has benefitted greatly from the comments of those who heard it. Convinced that mutual understanding is indispensible for Christian reunion, my main aim was to set forth briefly the position of the Episcopal Church on Baptism, some of the background thereof, some other contemporary views, and what seem to me the requirements of any contemporary statement of the doctrine of Baptism.

Since one is inevitably affected far more deeply than one appreciates by the strongest influences to which one has been exposed, it is only fair to readers to make plain what those influences have been. I was born and brought up an Episcopalian, one parent being an Anglo Catholic and the other an Evangelical; my family parish represented the middle-of-the-road type of Episcopalianism; my headmaster for six years, who was one of the strongest influences in my life, was a Broadchurchman.

2. All Christians agree that Baptism is the rite by which people are admitted into the Church. Therefore, *the importance which folks attach to Baptism depends on the importance they attach to the Church:* what we say about that Sacrament witnesses to our faith about the Church.

Underlying this paper are certain convictions about the Church widely, but not universally, held by Christians. (a) That the Church is basically a community (i.e. a structured life or a body with an immanent spirit) rather than simply an organization. The tie by which the Church is held together is a shared life of which the Giver and Lord is the Holy Spirit. (This conviction is part of

107

the Catholic heritage.) The life in which members of the Church participate is characterized by such things as a *common* trust in God as revealed in Christ; a *common* faith about the nature of God and about the nature and destiny of man; *common* worship, both sacramental and non-sacramental, both liturgical and free; *common* ethical norms; a *common* sense of mission; common aspirations and goals; *growth* in all these respects; and the like. This view of the Church is the same as that of the Archbishop of Canterbury in his widely quoted Cambridge University sermon. (b) That as baptism initiates people into the Christian community or shared life, so the Holy Communion is both the expression of the existing Christian community and also a powerful instrument for deepening it; and that intercommunion, therefore, may properly be permitted by the competent authorities of two or more Churches before they have achieved organizational amalgamation. This is a conviction widely held by Protestants within the Catholic tradition. (c) That in proportion as the community or Church grows in cohesiveness and in awareness of its mission, it will put forth the organization and the activities proper to its developing common life; formulae for expressing the common faith, forms of worship, constitutional and governmental structure, boards of missions, education, social service, finance, and so forth.

3. The purpose of this paper is not to consider baptism per se but Baptism in relation to Church unity. Hence, there is no need for us to consider the pre-Christian actors which have had some effect on the practice or doctrine of baptism—e.g. the Mystery Religion's rites of initiation and purification.

Nor need we consider John's baptism beyond remarking that: (a) Jesus evidently thought that baptism as taught and practiced by him was in some sense continuous with what John did. This is clear from his submission to John's rite. (b) The early Church also regarded its rites as a continuation of what the Baptist had done. Otherwise it would not have recorded so carefully both what John did and that Jesus submitted to it. (c) The early Church was even more impressed by the difference between the significance of John's baptism and of the Christian sacrament.

Nor is it necessary to go at length into the authority for continuing the rite today, though this is being much canvassed now. Suffice it to say that: (a) It is impossible to *prove* that our Lord used the exact words recorded in Matthew 28:16-20. A good many leading scholars think it probable that this precise form of words became standardized from the liturgical practice of the early Church. (cp. Quick, *The Christian Sacraments.*) (b) But one of the most thorough recent studies of the matter (Evans, *Sacraments in the New Testament with Special Reference to Baptism,* London, The Tyndale Press, 1946) argues that the odds are very strong that our Lord did command the use of these words; and that therefore the sanction behind the continuous administration of baptism in the name of the Father and of the Son and of the Holy Ghost, rather than in the name of Jesus only, is the command of Christ. Without pretending to New Testament scholarship, I am not entirely persuaded that Evans has made his point.

II. *Some Early, Medieval and Reformation Views*

It is worth reminding ourselves what was thought of Baptism by Paul (and other New Testament writers) and by the two most important pre-Reformation writers on the subject, Augustine and Aquinas, and by the chief Reformers.

1. It seems to me that Dodd is right in his interpretation of Romans 6:1-14. Paul is not concerned to argue the theology of Baptism. He *assumes* the rite and his interpretation thereof, and then uses this meaning (which must have been generally acceptable or his use of the ceremony would have been meaningless) for pedagogical purposes. Baptism is the "sacramental initiation into the Christian life!" it "involves the death of the old sinful self and the emergence of a new self." It is an "act by which the believer enters into all that Christ did and suffered as his Representative, in that 'He was delivered up for our trespasses and raised that we might be justified.'" (Dodd, *The Epistle to the Romans,* pp. 85-87.)

People were incorporated into the Church by the sacrament of baptism in virtue of their faith. Baptism was of adults, believers: belief and Baptism always went together. (Because believers "experienced all that Christ did and suffered for them, baptism into the Body of Christ meant a real sharing of His death and resurrection" (Dodd, p. 91) : it was not always merely a *picture* of participation therein, but sometimes was a means of accomplishing it.) Furthermore, membership in the Body of Christ was inseparable from the gift of the Spirit of Christ. Like the laying on of hands, baptism was sometimes administered before and sometimes after the reception of the Spirit. I know nothing which definitely shows the relation between Baptism, the laying on of hands and the gifts of the Spirit. Again, Paul regarded Baptism as an assurance of life beyond the grave; and therefore it was a great incentive to living as became a member of Christ's Body, or, in Augustine's phrase, to "Become what you are."

All Paul's thought of Baptism was conditioned by his thought of grace, and the chief difference between what he said about Baptism and what later writers said on the same subject goes back to a change in the understanding of grace. Throughout the New Testament grace is indistinguishable from the Gift of the Spirit; the evidence is overwhelming that grace "refers to the being and action of God as revealed and actualized in Jesus Christ, for He is in His person and work the self-giving of God. . . . Grace is identical with Jesus Christ in person and work and deed. . . . Later theology thought of *charis* as a divine attribute." (Torrance, *The Doctrine of Grace in the Apostolic Fathers,* p. 21, published 1948.) Baptism, then, is God's action.

2. Following Paul, Augustine put primary stress on baptism as a means whereby people are incorporated into the Church. Emphasis was laid also on the forgiveness of sin, both actual and original, as a result of baptism. (*Enchiridion,* ch. 42, 43, 50; *On the Creed,* ch. 15, 16; *On Continence,* ch. 386, etc.) It is arguable that faith was no longer regarded as the cause of the sacrament's efficacy, but that either correct performance of the rite brought the forgiveness of original sin or that the predestining grace of God saved people from exclusion from the Kingdom of Heaven. The fact that the rite was by this time very often administered to children forced some change in his thought about Baptism, and his predestinarian outlook furthered this alteration. Augustine wrote

freely about Baptism, but I cannot discover any uniform doctrine about it.

3. Aquinas (*Summa, Quest* LXII, LXIII) insisted that sacraments caused grace. Baptism conferred "character": it was the seal placed upon His own by Christ, as the king puts a brand on his soldiers, and that seal was the aptitude for rendering true Christian worship. By grace we die to the oldness of sin and begin to live a new life, the life of grace. By Baptism we are incorporated into the passion and death of Christ and freed from the debt of punishment due for past sin and by it we are incorporated into Christ and freed from the debt of punishment due for past sin and by it we are incorporated into Christ as His members and so, by the infusion of grace, are born into the spiritual life, enlightened by Christ with the knowledge of the truth, and made fruitful unto good works.

Baptism then, affects the individual who receives it; it is fundamentally a transaction between God and the individual which affects his status and capacities, and almost secondarily his incorporation into the whole company of the Church.

4. Luther laid great store by Baptism. He allowed only it and the Lord's Supper as sacraments, because to be a sacrament a rite must have been instituted by Christ. In his anxiety to avoid restricting Baptism to believers, as did the Anabaptists, he wavered between ascribing the Sacrament's efficacy to the incipient faith of the baptized infant and ascribing it to the faith of the sponsor. Both these views made the rite far more individualistic than he liked, so increasingly he emphasized it as initiation into the Christian community. Baptism was efficacious because of God's act, not because of any human deserts. It "effects the remission of sins, frees us from death and the devil, and gives blessedness and everlasting life to those who believe what the word and the promises of God declare" (*Short Catechism,* p. 14, *Luther's Primary Works,* transl. Wace & Buchheim, 1896.) cp. also *The Greater Catechism,* p. 129-143; *The Treatise on Baptism,* p. 41-71; *The Babylonian Captivity,* p. 218-245; The *Baptismal Office,* p. 193-211, vol. 6 in 6 vol. Edition of Luther's works. Kramm, *The Theology of*

Martin Luther, 1947, p. 52-55. Bainton, *Here I Stand,* pp. 136-142. Publ. 1950.

5. Calvin (*Institutes,* Bk. IV, XIV and XV) thought a sacrament was "an outward sign by which the Lord seals in our consciences the promises of His goodwill towards us to support the weakness of our faith; and we on our part testify our piety to Him . . . as well as before other men, a testimony of the grace of God towards us, confirmed by an outward sign, with a reciprocal attestation of our piety toward Him." Baptism "is a sign of initiation by which we are admitted into the society of the Church in order that, being incorporated into Christ, we may be numbered among the children of God." It greatly assists our faith because it has the warrant of Christ's command, its effects are permanent, it incites us to virtue, it so ingrafts us into the life and death of Christ as to make us partakers of all His benefits, it assures us that we have Christ's promise of the remission of our sins.

III. *Some Anglican Teaching*

1. *The Book of Common Prayer*

(a) Baptism and spiritual rebirth together result in remission of sin:—"he, coming to thy holy baptism, may receive remission of sin by spiritual regeneration." This reproduces the teaching of Paul and the Fourth Gospel that the sacrament is very important, and also that beside the rite, rebirth and the Holy Spirit are necessary for entrance into the Kingdom of God. Neither is emphasized over the other: all are said to be requisite for the Kingdom. (It is to be remembered that among the purposes of the Fourth Evangelist was to make it clear that the external rite was futile unless it was accompanied by the profound inner change designated by the term "rebirth," a point made against the incipient external formalism and the infiltration of quasi-magical ideas that characterized Mystery Cults.)

(b) By Baptism and spiritual regeneration God grafts candidates into His Church; and this membership is the basis upon which we are exhorted to live the life that becomes those who have died to the old way and been raised to the new. Church membership is the vitally important result of rebirth by water and the Spirit.

The Offices of Instruction (as formerly did the Catechism) slightly vary the emphasis of the Office of Baptism by showing the first and primary result of the Sacrament to be Church membership. In it one is made "a member of Christ, a child of God and an inheritor of the Kingdom of Heaven." Now, I think it probable that the compilers and revisers of the Prayer Book interpreted the phrase "I was made a member of Christ," in a Pauline sense of "a member of the Church," a sense which seems to have been held by both Augustine and Aquinas. (To be sure, "a member of Christ" was a more inclusive phrase than "a member of the Church." The former phrase included also the idea that people were personally attached directly to the Lord Himself as well as to the others who, by their attachment to Him, were also attached to one another. But equally certain the phrase "a member of Christ" included Church membership.)

(c) The Twenty-seventh Article of Religion gives the same teaching as the Catechism—that Baptism is a sign of a Christian man's profession, an instrument whereby people are grafted into the Church, the seal of the promises of their forgiveness and adoption as sons of God. By Baptism faith is confirmed, and grace is increased by prayer. (The teaching of this article is very similar to that of John Calvin, and through him, of the Presbyterian Church. Much like it, also, is the official teaching of Methodism.)

2. To save time I shall skip both Jewel and the Caroline divines, because, despite their great interest, they add nothing of substance on baptism that is not in Hooker. He contended against the Puritans on various details, but underlying other differences were (a) their biblical literalism (that is, everything taught in Scripture must be forever observed and nothing not so enjoined might be practiced at all, for example, the sign of the Cross in Baptism); (b) their rigid predestinarianism, which prevented Baptism from being regarded as a means of grace, to which he replied that he believed *ex animo* in predestination but not in determinism. (God left men free to accept or reject the destiny He set before them, and Baptism is a means of grace to accept their destiny. cp. Hooker,

113

Bks. II & III, and his essay on predestination.) The gist of Hooker's teaching is: (a) Though people can be saved apart from sacraments, Christ desiring them to be baptized as a means whereby grace is received, and such saving Baptism must be by both water and the Spirit. It is man's part not to argue about this but to obey Christ' will. (b) Men must not be too rigorous but remember that the inward gift *may* be enjoyed even though the outward rite is lacking, for the saving reality is always God's gift and men's desire to do God's will. (c) Grace is not absolutely tied to Baptism, for unbaptized infants may be saved. "Wherefore, a necessity there is of receiving, and a necessity of administering, the sacrament of baptism; the one peradventure not so absolute as some have thought, but out of all peradventure the other more straight and narrow than that the Church, which is by office a Mother into such as crave at her hands the sacred mystery of new birth, should repel them and see them die unsatisfied of their ghostly desires rather than give them their soul's right with the omission of those things that serve only but for the more convenient and orderly administration thereof." (LX 7) Baptism in the name of the Trinity is ordinarily necessary for salvation, and Baptism of the Spirit always is necessary.

All that I have written so far is common to Methodists and Episcopalians. Most of it is equally true of the tradition of Lutherans and Presbyterians.

3. After the Restoration the later Latitudinarians were amazingly careless about Baptism, and not unnaturally the Evangelicals reacted strongly against them and insisted on the necessity and privilege of administering and receiving the rite. Very strong differences as to its meaning were thought to be argued by Pusey's tract, *On Baptism,* published in 1835 (most important in its expanded form), and by C. S. Gorham. Both of them wrote one-sidedly. Reading them today one finds it difficult to imagine why either of their views caused much excitement. The "Baptismal Controversy" is a notable example of how the temper of an age produces misunderstanding and misrepresentation. With great learning Dr. Pusey argued that Baptism was necessary, that it was a means of grace, that it brought forgiveness and membership in the

114

body of Christ, that it must be taken seriously and strict discipline enforced. Gorham was tried for heresy in 1848, maintaining that Baptism did not per se confer grace or save a man without faith, but that conversion was essential, and was acquitted by the Judicial Committee of the Privy Council on the grounds that his teaching was legitimate in the Church of England. Neither he nor Pusey taught anything novel or contradictory to the Prayer Book.

4. (a) No Anglican theologian has made so much of Baptism as F. D. Maurice. Homiletically, it was the basis of his appeal to Christian living—now being regenerate children of God, Christians should live as became their status. Ecclesiologically, it symbolized the difference between membership in the Universal Church and a sect, and it revealed the sectarianism of many ardent churchmen. Theologically, it illustrated the basic Christian doctrines. Cp. esp. *The Kingdom of Christ,* II, Ch. 4, p. 261-291 (Everyman edition), *Theological Essays,* p. 162 ff.; autobiography by his son; several volumes of sermons *passim,* esp. *Christmas Day & Other Sermons;* Alec Vidler, *Witness to the Light,* Ch. 4 (1948).

(b) Baptism, Maurice thought, is the sign and pledge to those who receive it that they have the inward grace of being united to God and to one another in Christ. It is the sacrament of initiation into a relationship established by God's act and not by their own desires, virtues or action. It is, secondly, the declaration of the true law of man's being, a divine act assuring him that he is His child and not the devil's (against any theory of total depravity) and evil only when he ignores his true nature and believes the devil's lie that he belongs to him. Thirdly, Baptism tells men that God has remitted their sins, that they may approach at all times their Father Who has redeemed them and reconciled them to Himself in Christ and in Christ has made them heirs of eternal life; and all this He has done solely because of His love. This is simply Maurice's expansion of the declaration that the baptized are "members of Christ, children of God and inheritors of the Kingdom of Heaven." Baptism is fundamentally the initiation into a permanent and constant relationship.

Vidler suggests (*Witness to the Light,* p. 106) that the best statement of what Maurice meant was given by F. W. Robertson

115

in a sermon wherein he likened Baptism to coronation. Coronation cannot make a man king unless he is already sovereign by reason of being the son of the previous king, so Baptism cannot make a person a child of God unless God has already adopted him as His son. But coronation, the event from which all royal acts date, adds authority to the fact (his sovereignty) which was a fact before coronation. So Baptism is God's authoritative declaration in material form of what was already a spiritual reality, i.e. that the candidate is God's child.

(c) Baptism is no private endowment of grace to a particular individual (against both the Catholics and Evangelicals of Maurice's day) but the establishment of a man in the Church. This puts him into the right relationship with God and men. To have this happen to one is so significant that it is like being born again or regenerated. In Christ *mankind* was reborn, a new race of men begun of which He is the first fruit. Baptism asserts that each recipient of the sacrament, by being incorporated into this new race, shares in that rebirth of mankind.

5. *Doctrine in the Church of England* (p. 136-139) adds nothing about Baptism to what I have already mentioned in one place or another, but it is an admirable statement of the effects of that Sacrament—spiritual cleansing through "incorporation into the church, the fellowship of the redeemed, in which the Holy Spirit as given through the revelation of God in Christ is at work," carrying the promise of purification from the evil in 'the world'; committing those who have been cleansed to a life-long struggle with evil: effects which are eternal as is the Church into which it admits them. It also deals well with the difficult questions raised by infant Baptism.

6. The Lambeth Conference, 1948, emphasized: (a) the inseparable connection between the ministry of the Word and of the Sacraments (was this an oblique attack on Rome?); (b) the importance of infant Baptism as part of the candidate's total initiation into the Christian life, and therefore the fundamental connection between baptism, confirmation and holy communion; (c) the insistence that the gift of grace is to be understood as the operation and influence of the Holy Spirit upon the Spirit of man

116

(against any mechanical theory of grace) and that the activity of the Spirit is not limited to the Church.

IV. *Some Methodist Teaching*

1. The fundamental law of Methodism consists of the Articles of Religion, The General Rules, the Articles of Organization and Government. The Articles of Organization and Government, Article X, section 1, states: "The General Conference shall not revoke, alter nor change our Articles of Religion, nor establish any new standards or rules of doctrine contrary to our present existing and established standards of doctrine."

These standards of doctrine are the Articles of Religion, and these, in turn, are the Thirty-Nine Articles reduced to twenty-five with various changes. The omitted Articles are III, VIII, IX after the words "is of his own nature inclined to evil," XIII, XV, XVII, XVIII, XIX second paragraph, XXI, XXIII, XXVI, XXIX, XXXIII, XXXV, XXXVI. There are also some changes of words and phrases. It seemed clear that the reasons for these changes were (a) clarification of Elizabethan wording; (b) elimination of what Wesley thought to be unprovable statements, e.g. that the Nicene Creed "may be proved by most certain warrants of Holy Scripture"; (c) elimination of anything that smacked of determinism, or that minimized human responsibility and the requirements of holiness; (d) elimination of anything that minimized justification by grace; (e) elimination of anything that could be taken to imply the necessity of English or Anglican ways.

2. The only Article dealing with baptism is numbered XXVII in the Prayer Book and XVII in Wesley's version. It differs, in addition to a verbal change, from the Prayer Book Article by omitting everything between "whereby as by an instrument—by virtue of prayer unto God." That is, it omits all reference to baptism as an effective instrument and leaves it entirely as a sign.

In the Methodist Ritual (strongly recommended but not mandatory), all the services of baptism (infant, children, youth, adults) strongly urge that the rite be administered in the church building at the regular service; and permit immersion or pouring or sprin-

117

kling, in the Triune Name. Each of the services is a sign, not an instrument, not a symbol which effects what it symbolizes: this is the major difference between the Methodist and Episcopal forms.

3. But several qualifications to this last statement are needed. (i) Baptism admits to the Church and gives a name and (ii) Baptism consecrates the recipient "to God and to His Church"; to this extent it is an instrument. (iii) The parents and sponsors undertake that the child will be taught "the meaning and purpose of this holy sacrament," as well as the Christian faith and the nature of the Christian life, etc. As a result of such training and of the steady prayers for growth in grace, he may become a "worthy member of Christ's holy Church." Such teaching and training indicates faith that God has done something which makes the growth possible: rebirth is the natural implication. (iv) Everything significant in the life of Christians is ascribed to the activity of the Holy Spirit. Thus, to the Sacrament is ascribed some of the effect ascribed to it in all periods of the Church; and there is also an unwillingness similar to the hesitancy of more traditional days to be too sure just what produces spiritual results.

V. *Other Non-Anglican Teaching*

1. The Orthodox Church, according to Gavin, (*Greek Orthodox Thought*, 1923, pp. 306-323), holds that "Baptism is the sacrament in which he who is thrice immersed in the Name of the Father and of the Son and of the Holy Ghost, is cleansed from all sin and regenerated spiritually" (quoting Dyobouniotes *Ta Mysteria*, p. 38), and is the door into the Church and into participation in the other sacraments. Three-fold immersion and the invocation of the Trinity and the proper formula are indispensable minima of a valid Baptism. Normally it must be at the hands of a bishop or priest but since Baptism is "absolutely necessary for all" except those who have witnessed to the faith by martyrdom, it may be administered *in extremis* by laymen. Baptism effects the forgiveness of sin, both original and actual, and regenerates and illuminates the soul, and makes the recipient an heir of salvation by adoption. The fact that it produces results *ex opere operato* is the reason why it is properly administered to unconscious infants (and

I suppose to unconscious adults also). A valid Baptism can no more be repeated than physical birth, not (as the Romans say) because of any theory of indelibility but because of the nature of the sacrament. Anyone who has been baptized twice, even though it was done in ignorance, is barred from Holy Orders.

Baptism is completed and perfected by the sacrament of Chrism, or anointing with consecrated oil. This is performed by a priest, the oil being consecrated by the bishop. It is performed immediately after Baptism, and separation of these two sacraments is entirely unjustifiable. Orthodox scholars admit that dominical institution of Chrism cannot be proved. It confers the Holy Spirit. This gift may have been given originally by the laying on of hands; but gradually the laying on of hands was dropped, probably because there were too few bishops to administer it to so many people so widely scattered. (P. 320. Gavin cites approvingly various authorities who held to this as the most probable reason.)

2. (a) The Confession of Faith, adopted in 1729 and amended in 1788 and 1903 by the Presbyterian Church U.S.A., states the official doctrinal position of that Church and, I believe, of all churches holding the Reformed system. It is in harmony with the Larger and Shorter Catechisms.

(b) The Confession states that Baptism was ordained by Christ, is to be continued unto the end of the world, admits to the visible church, is a sign and seal of the covenant of grace, of the recipient's ingrafting into Christ, of his regeneration, of the remission of sins and of his dedication to Christ: It is to be administered by water (either by dipping or sprinkling) in the Triune Name by a minister. Baptism is not to be restricted to those who personally profess faith, but is to be administered also to children of parents one or both of whom are believers. But salvation is not so inseparably annexed to Baptism that no person can be regenerated or saved without it, or that everyone who is baptized is automatically saved. The saving grace of Baptism is both exhibited and conferred by the Holy Ghost on all to whom God has appointed that grace.

(c) We note that the Confession differs from the Episcopal Offices of Baptism and Instruction chiefly in the following points. (1) At least one parent must be a professed believer, (2) The sacrament must be administered by a minister. I understand that these requirements are due (i) to a desire to safeguard Baptism from profanation; (ii) to ensure that parents, those who by nature will have the chief influence over children, bring them up in the nurture and admonition of the Lord.

3. Baptism has again become a vital and extremely controversial subject among many contemporary European Protestants, as two examples will show.

(a) Karl Barth's *The Teaching of the Church Concerning Baptism* is the "most serious challenge to infant baptism which has ever been offered." (Cullmann, *Baptism in the New Testament,* English edition, 1950, p. 8.) He regards it as a "wound in the body of Christ." He argues that the constitutive act of Baptism, that which makes certain words and deeds a once-for-all and unrepeatable acts of grace, is *cognitio,* or the response of faith to knowledge imparted about Christ's death and resurrection. It is obviously impossible to impart such knowledge to infants because they cannot understand what is being said, and for the same reason they cannot respond by faith; therefore, to go through the form of baptizing is perilously close to magic or blasphemy. Barth evidently thinks that "faith and confession are preconditions to significant and regular Baptism." (P. 28.)

(b) Cullmann's book is in part a very learned refutation of Barth's thesis and defense of infant Baptism. His main points are: (i) God wrought salvation for *mankind* by the death and resurrection of Christ, and participation in Christ's death and resurrection he sometimes designates as "general Baptism." (ii) God has wrought the incorporation of *individuals* into the Body of Christ by what he sometimes calls simply "Baptism," sometimes "Church Baptism," sometimes "Christian Baptism." The fundamental thing about (Church or Christian Baptism) is that by that action the individual is made a member of the Church: this act seals or "stamps" him a participant in the new covenant. (iii) The recipient of Church Baptism has a purely passive role—the action is all God's. If the person is properly baptized, God places him within the Church even though he be unconscious (as an infant is) or not yet a believer (as children are). (iv) But the Church properly requires a confession of faith before administering adult Baptism, as a sign of the candidate's personal faith in the Church and, consequently, an earnest of his perseverance in the community. (v) And faith is a necessary consequence to Baptism, for though lack of faith cannot impair the reality of the Church Baptism, permaent lack of faith or complete loss of faith entails loss of participation in Christ's death and resurrection. To participate in the Church is to be in a state of grace, and whether a man remains in that state of grace depends on his action after baptism. (Another theological statement by Aulen, a great Swedish scholar, is of fundamentally this same view. Cp. *The Faith of the Christian Church,* pp. 353 ff. second English edition, 1948.) He contends that far from being a less worthy form than adult, infant baptism is "the highest, purest and most perfect form" of the sacrament.

4. The most interesting study of the sacraments by any contemporary Protestant is Paul Tillich's *The Protestant Era,* chapter VIII. Influenced deeply by German and American thought and practice, possessing extraordinary learning and penetration, he has brought together the insight of the Bible, Augustine and classical Protestantism (especially in its Lutheran form) that salvation is the unmerited gift of God appropriated solely by personal trust in Him, the insights of the Greeks and the Renaissance that truth is more important than any particular formulation thereof, and that no human activity may be excluded from the Church's purview save only sin, the insights of modern psychological, sociological and historical students. He argues:

(a) The natural objects have inherent capacity which enables them to be bearers of transcendent power, either divine or demonic. They are potential sacraments. An object or event is sacramental if the power is controlled by God; it is demonic if that power is controlled by some human agency.

(b) That there is a "necessary relationship" in a sacrament between the material element and the particular grace-gift. The sacrament of Baptism is possible because water has an inherent power of its own by virtue of which it "is suited to become the bearer of sacral power and thus also to become a sacramental element" whereby forgiveness is conveyed, or a death to sin and a new birth unto righteousness. Tillich rejects the idea that Baptism (or the Lord's Supper) is simply a dramatic representation of the meaning of the sacrament, not only because this is untrue to the main stream of Christian experience but also because it disregards the modern scientific teaching that "even in the structure of the atom there is something primordial, a Gestalt, an intrinsic power." (*Protestant Era,* p. 100) Baptism (and the Lord's Supper) effects what it symbolizes. Likewise, he rejects the "nominalistic" view that the elements can convey grace only because God so commanded. Why did God ordain water (or bread or wine) rather than something else? Why, except that each of those elements had some inherent power which not only made it appropriate for use in the Sacrament but inevitable?

(c) That a word "like other natural elements, can become part of a ritual act in which it functions as the bearer of transcendent power: it can become sacramental." (p. 98) As an example of this he cites the words of absolution.

(d) Water (or bread and wine, or the words of absolution) have the inherent capacity to become bearers of divine powers, but they become so *in fact* only if they are related to the events by which salvation was wrought, and they are so related if they are used in faith by the Church acting through its appropriate agents. One constant danger is that of thinking that the material element *is* the divine power rather than the bearer of such power.

(e) The essential thing about our Lord is not particular words or acts but the new sort of life, the life perfectly related to God and, therefore, to other people and to nature, which He manifested in His total career. By having this life Himself He began it for the race and enabled people to enter into it by faith and to develop in it by the help of the sacraments. One might say that there had evolved upon earth the *genus homo:* Our Lord began the *genus christianum.*

(f) Tillich says nothing about Baptism as incorporation into the Church. This is not because he disbelieves it but because he takes it for granted and concentrates his attention on the relation between nature, grace and sacraments.

Tillich ardently professes Protestantism, but much of his thought is Catholic, and he is steeped in the spirit of Christian Humanism. It is precisely because of this combination that his thought has more in common with the main stream of Anglicanism than any other Protestant leader.

VI. *Conclusion*

A doctrine of Baptism must include the following affirmation:

1. *Baptism is the sacrament of* Church initiation, the rite by which people are incorporated into the Church. Since "sacraments are the self-impartation of divine love in the form of action" (Aulen, op. cit. p. 370), Baptism of helpless infants is a peculiarly appropriate piece of symbolism. Through membership in the Great Society, they participate in the destiny God has set before them with all its unsearchable riches, of which riches the chief are the Holy Spirit and eternal life. My major thesis is that *Baptism is a sacrament, an instrument by which God conveys His grace to men, precisely because it is the action by which people are incorporated into the Church.* Since God is love, to become part of the fellowship that is the creation of His love is to receive His grace. Lest anyone think that by stressing this incorporation as the key to a correct understanding of the rite I undervalue it, I record my agreement with Maurice's tremendous statement (*Theological Essays* 3rd edition, p. 205) that the great heresy and sin for which Rome will have to give account is its failure properly to estimate the Church, for Rome makes it a sect based on agreement with the opinion of a group, rather than the Universal Church based on the activity of God. (Cp. Maurice, *Theological Essays* 3rd edition, p. 205.)

Admission to the Church is of great importance, furthermore, because to a large extent our growth in grace or sin is due to the folk who influence us. The people who, because they attract or repel us and, consequently, affect our opinions and tastes, our convictions and morals, form the spiritual environment which is the primary factor governing our development. Because human beings are so profoundly affected by many men and women of whose role in their lives they are unaware, it is of vast moment to have a constructive Christian circle of acquaintances. Membership in the Church means (at least in theory) formative exposure to the spiritual environ-

123

ment created by a particular local Christian group and to the wider influence of the larger Christian society. The people by whom Christian influence is first mediated are parents—they are the earliest ministers of Christ. Later many other people are involved, including those who write books, but always it is the words and deeds of some persons that create the spiritual environment which makes people more Christian or less so—and behind them is the Holy Spirit. The Church, "the fellowship of Christ's religion," is of incalculable importance. Baptism is a sacrament that mediates forgiveness, because it is the rite by which we are incorporated into the Christian fellowship.

Three deductions follow from the influence exerted by people among whom children are brought up: (i) That the value of sponsorship has been largely nullified because people are often asked to be god-parents to pay them a social compliment. (ii) That the carelessnesss with which most people treat their responsibilities as sponsors fully justifies those Churches which omit sponsors entirely, thinking it wiser to put the responsibility for the religious nurture of children entirely on the parents and elders. (iii) That baptism should almost always be held at regular services, partly because this is the way of illustrating vividly that baptism is the act of initiation into the Church, and partly because such public christenings may teach the congregation its responsibility for exerting a definite Christian influence on its child members.

2. *Baptism is the sacrament of attachment:* The outward and visible sign of the inward and spiritual grace of divine love. Therefore baptism unites Christianity's irreducible individualism and its ineradicable corporate stress. The same act that marks a person as God's simultaneously grafts him into the Church. In Baptism the child is given a name. The name stands for the whole person and for his difference from every other person, and for his involvement in the community which requires the name as a means of identification. When the Church names a helpless infant, the participants witness that God cares for him just as he is, that he is a distinct personality (at least potentially) and that he can become his full self only as he appropriates the resources, and grows into the responsibilities, of life in a Christian community.

124

Christianity teaches that God desires every person to grow into an increasingly distinct individual, and also to become ever more inextricably attached to others—as an iron filing is attached to the magnet and also to other iron filings, as a branch is organically bound to the trunk and all the branches. It becomes as hard to detach the filings from one another as from the magnet—magnet and filings become one magnetized mass. So Christians attached individually to God in Christ are thereby attached to one another as a united group, and this united group, which is the Church, becomes increasingly an agent for drawing and attaching other people to the Lord. Furthermore, as the force that attracts iron filings and binds them together is something entirely other than the objects attracted, so the power that draws and unites people is something quite other than the people thus drawn, being the Spirit who is love and who proceedeth from the Father and the Son (i.e. who is integral to the ultimate reality) and who works chiefly through people. But the word "attachment" connotes affection as well as impersonal bond: what relates people to each other is from one point of view their subjective mutual regard. The divine love which is God's Holy Spirit going forth *to* them is also God's Spirit *in* them. Baptism is the sacrament of attachment.

To say the same thing somewhat differently, Baptism is the perpetual mark and pledge of God's love for the individuals who have been baptized; it is the mark that they who have received it belong to God rather than to the spirit of evil, even as a brand marked a soldier as belonging to the emperor or a slave to its master. It is their guarantee that the nature of Ultimate Power is self-giving love such as was manifested by the Crucified.

3. *Baptism is the chief sacrament of Christian unity,* primarily because it is the most universal sacrament of Christian love. All Protestant Churches recognize one another's christenings; even Rome regards as valid a Protestant baptism if the competent authority is satisfied that all the necessities have been met, and rebaptizes only on the ground that some indispensable factor may have been omitted. Baptism, at least in theory, unites all Christians.

In the *Proposed Basis of Unions* the Presbyterian and Episcopal representatives agreed: "The two Sacraments ordained by Christ,

125

Baptism and the Supper of the Lord, are sure witnesses to the mighty acts of God and are means of grace appropriated by faith. Baptism is a sign and seal of God's covenant in Christ, of ingrafting into Him, of remission of sins by His death, of regeneration by His Spirit, and of incorporation into His Church." This sentence reveals how closely the two groups agreed regarding Baptism. Methodists and Lutherans and several other Communions would likewise agree to it. How much of a bond between those groups that Sacrament is!

CHAPTER X

Constitutional Issues

by CHARLES C. PARLIN

My assignment is a ten minute paper on possible procedures toward organic union. The paper is to serve as a basis for discussion.

Discussions can be premised on these accepted principles:

First: Both Churches have expressed unequivocally desire for some unity.

Second: It is not intended or expected that either Church will merely absorb into itself the other.

Third: We are considering a procedure which will combine so far as possible the heritages of both Churches and which will result in one church with one standard of faith, one ministry, one communicant list, one system of government.

Fourth: We can expect to produce no plan which will please all members of both Churches.

Fifth: No plan should be consummated, however, unless it carries the overwhelming support of both Churches; otherwise we would end with one new Church and two old ones: three churches where we have now only two and thus defeat our purpose —unity.

Sixth: Our hope for carrying overwhelming support of both Churches must be based on careful cultivation and education of the two memberships.

From the standpoint of corporate law the procedures are relatively clear. There must be a Plan of Union. We may assume that this would require amendments to the Constitutions of both Churches.

The Methodist action on such plan would follow its Constitution, Division II, Section III(2). The proposal may originate either in the General Conference itself or come to it from some Annual Conference. In the General Conference the proposal must receive a 2/3 majority of all present and voting and then be referred back to the Annual Conferences where it must receive a 2/3 majority of all members of the several Annual Conferences present and voting. Each Annual Conference is composed of the ordained ministers of the conference and one layman elected from each church in the conference.

The Episcopal action on the plan would be by its General Convention. The plan would require the 2/3 vote of the House of Bishops and a 2/3 vote of the House of Deputies, voting by orders. If so adopted the plan would not become effective but it would be sent out to each diocese of review. Then at the next General Convention it would come up again and, if again adopted by a 2/3 vote of each House, the House of Deputies again voting by orders, the Plan would become effective. The House of Bishops is composed of all active and retired Bishops, each of whom has one vote. The House of Deputies is composed of deputies, half lay and half clergy, elected by the diocese. Voting in the House of Deputies is by dioceses.

Favorable action by the two Churches would be followed by a uniting conference composed of delegates duly elected and instructed by their respective Churches. We recognize, of course, that both the drafting of such a plan of union and the preparation for its presentation to the supreme governing bodies of the two present Churches would take much careful and consecrated work. We now merely discuss possible procedural steps, assuming that organic union is our ultimate objective.

On procedures I have reviewed three union efforts in which one or the other of our churches has been recently involved:

I. *The Methodist plan of union of three denominations consummated in 1939.* I find in this the problems so different as to render little guidance in our present situation. It was all within the Methodist family. The Methodist Protestant group had broken away in 1828 largely on the issue of the episcopacy and in reuniting they accepted episcopacy in the present Methodist form. The Church North and South had split in 1844 largely on the issue of slavery. The Church North had Negro membership and congregations but the Church South finally solved their problem by establishing for the Negroes a separate denomination—the Colored Methodist Episcopal Church. Basis for union was found in the establishment of the system of Jurisdictions within the Methodist Church, one of these Jurisdictions being exclusively Negro.

II. *The current Conferences on Church Union among eight churches which recognize a common ministry, in which the Methodists are participants and the Episcopalians are observers.* This effort originated in informal discussions, after the failure of the Episcopal-Presbyterian efforts, premised at least in part on the theory that movements toward Church union in the United States could not, and should not, be delayed until the Episcopal Church was in position to move toward union. These discussions culminated in a call to a Conference at Seabury House, Greenwich, Conn., December 14-16, 1949. At this conference the following eight denominations agreed to explore together the possibility of union:

> African Methodist Episcopal Zion
> Colored Methodist Episcopal
> Congregational Christian
> Disciples of Christ
> Evangelical and Reformed
> Methodist
> Presbyterian U.S.
> Presbyterian U.S.A.

The International Council of Community Churches is also represented. The Protestant Episcopal Church participates as an observer. A proposed plan of union has gone through several drafts. A draft was considered by a full meeting of the respective Commissions for the first time at Cincinnati in January, 1951, and referred back to the drafting committee. The drafting committee has met once in New York since and is scheduled to meet again in New Hampshire for the week beginning July 2, 1951. Here again, I find no particular help as to pattern. Oversimplified perhaps, the problem seems to be a conflict between the Congregational form of government and the Methodist form of episcopacy and

129

discipline. The present drafts call for recognition of an episcopacy with powers to appoint ministers within some limited scope but problems of reconciling Methodist order and discipline with congregationalism remain for the drafting committee. Title to church property will serve as an illustration of the difficulties. In churches of the congregational type the local church has title to its property and they say their individual congregations will not be willing to surrender this right. In the Methodist Church each local church deed must contain a provision that the property is held in trust for the denomination and Methodists are quite unwilling to surrender their properties back to the local churches. So the present draft tries to straddle the proposition by providing:

"In the case of a local church which holds title to its own property, the church retains the title. A local church now holding its property in trust for the denomination would transfer this trust from the denomination to the United Church."

Procedures, which is the subject matter of this paper, have not been adopted and are in fact only in very early stage of discussion.

III. *The efforts of the Episcopalians and the Presbyterians.* In this connection I have examined, among others, the following documents:

1. "Proposals Looking Toward Organic Union" issued jointly by the two Commissions in 1940.

2. "Basic Principles Proposed for the Union" issued jointly in 1943.

3. "Episcopal and Presbyterian Official Formularies of Doctrine Compared" issued in 1944 by the Committee on Church Unity of the Diocese of Michigan.

4. Report of the Episcopal Joint Commission to the General Convention of 1946.

5. "A Statement of Faith and Order" prepared by the Joint Commission for Submission to the Lambeth Conference. While the negotiations did not succeed, nevertheless I find in these materials much help and guidance.

The Methodist General Conference meets in San Francisco in May, 1952, and the Episcopal General Convention in Boston in

October, 1952. The question is whether once more our professions of a desire for unity shall take the form of merely an exchange of warm, fraternal greeting or will we have something ready to propose to these 1952 assemblies as a first step toward union?

We can probably dismiss summarily the prospect of having by that time any definitive plan for union.

The work of our Commissions would appear to fall into two categories: (1) what can be done between now and the time of the 1952 assemblies, and (2) what action should be prepared for, and recommended to, the 1952 assemblies.

Preliminary Work

It probably goes outside the intended scope of this paper to suggest subjects for interim studies. I was, however, impressed by the pamphlet *Episcopal and Presbyterian Formularies of Doctrine* issued by the Michigan Diocese. A similar study of Episcopal and Methodist doctrines and rituals would give a material which could be distributed widely and start the memberships thinking. I venture the guess that many laymen, conscious of certain divergencies of form, would be surprised and impressed to see how much the two Churches have in common, all taken of course from a common source.

When the Commissions are ready, materials on the ministries and the sacraments, and possible solutions for the problems which they present, might be put in pamphlet form available for study primarily by the clergy of the two churches.

A tabulation, for the use of the Commissions, of our areas of agreement and differences might be of help.

1952 Assemblies

In connection with the two assemblies of 1952 we should consider at least the following steps:

1. Report our conversations and meetings to date, in order that the Churches at large may know that this work is in process.

2. Ask that the respective Commissions be continued and that they be instructed to continue their work toward union.

3. Ask that any papers or pamphlet materials theretofore pre-

131

pared and in distribution be commended to the Churches for study.

4. Ask that in the various dioceses and annual conferences, committees on church unity be established. From the materials I have seen it appears that at least the Michigan Diocese has such a committee but I do not know how general that is in the Episcopal Church. I believe the Methodists have nothing of this type. Such committees could be useful in serving as contact points when the time comes for carrying any plan of union to the memberships of the churches generally.

5. We might consider asking authority, before the following scheduled meetings of the General Convention (1955) and the General Conference (1956), to call a large joint meeting of the two memberships for the purpose of considering and discussing a plan of union should our Commissions succeed in the drafting of one. The membership of such a large joint meeting might come from the "committees on unity" suggested above. I present this suggestion as a possibility because this procedure is being strongly urged by our congregationally minded brothers in the other negotiations. They convincingly point out that no plan of union can be successfully presented to a governing assembly unless it has wide and substantial support. They argue that Commissions and drafting committees themselves are numerically too few. Such large and preliminary meeting could be called for the specific and limited purpose of reviewing a plan of union proposed by the Commissions and reporting a recommendation to the General Convention of 1955 and the General Conference of 1956 respectively. The theory would be, for example, if the Episcopal wing of this larger meeting failed to recommend the plan there would be nothing to come before the General Convention; on the other hand, if this larger meeting did by convincing majority approve, it would seem reasonable to hope that the General Convention would accept.

6. And lastly, since the reading of Dean Kelley's paper and our discussion of last evening I add, for consideration, whether we could have ready for the 1952 assemblies any action, no matter how preliminary, looking toward inter-communion of our two churches as a step toward, rather than as a result or objective of, organic merger.

CHAPTER XI

The Body–Spirit Paradox of the Church

By REV. THEODORE O. WEDEL, Ph.D.

Ernest Troeltsch, in an article entitled "The Church" (*Religion in Geschichte und Gegenwart*) has this to say on the clash between Roman Catholic and Reformation doctrinal views: "The Reformation concept of the Church did not arise out of opposition to Catholic doctrine but out of opposition to Catholic practice. Even after Trent, or even after the Vatican Council, no systematic doctrine of the Church exists in Roman Catholic theology. What does exist is a cult which places the Church in the center of all Catholic piety."

An Eastern Orthodox scholar voices a similar judgment regarding the doctrine of the Church in the history of theology: "It is impossible to start with a formal definition of the Church. For, strictly speaking, there is none which could claim any doctrinal authority. None can be found in the Fathers nor in the Schoolmen, nor even in St. Thomas Aquinas." *

This absence of a complete dogmatic treatment of the Church, or this lack of dogmatic warfare regarding the Church, is surely one of the curiosities of Christian history. Christianity without the Church is unthinkable. Hence, until the Reformation, or even until our present ecumenical dilemma, Christians have generally taken the fellowship of faith within which they experienced the grace of the Gospel and the presence of the Lord, simply for granted. Particularly in the era of the Eastern and Western catholicisms, "it was easy to identify in practice the existing visible institution with the Body of Christ, and to say to the inquirer, 'if you wish to know the meaning and nature of the Church, look around you.' " **

The above observations pointing to a lack of doctrinal enlight-

---

* G. Florovsky, in *The Universal Church in God's Design*, p. 43.
** *The Fulness of Christ—A Report presented to His Grace the Archbishop of Canterbury* (London: S.P.C.K., 1950), page 30.

ment as regards the Church may seem at first to be exaggerated. Do not the Creeds define the Church as One, Holy, Catholic, and Apostolic? Are there not a whole series of metaphors and other verbal formulae in the New Testament descriptive of the Church which can receive doctrinal interpretation? At least three such hallowed phrases come to mind at once—Body of Christ, Communion of Saints, and Fellowship of the Holy Spirit. One must grant that of *biblical* material for the construction of a doctrine of the Church there is no lack, particularly if the biblical theme-song of "the people of God" in both Old and New Testaments is given full weight. The striking fact remains, however, that so little has really been made of this biblical material by the learned doctors. In place of doctrinal definitions of the Church, we have in its place what one might call "absolutised history." Fellowships of faith and cult have appeared on the historical scene, each one self-contained, experiencing the *fact* of Church-life from within. Each such communion has until recently at least taken the problem of inner unity very seriously.

The guarding of doctrinal orthodoxy and liturgical uniformity, and even ministerial succession can be traced in the story of every church, Catholic or Protestant, down to our era of ecumenical fraternization.

Seen from within, as a matter of fact, if we ignore the more extreme forms of sectarianism, the Churches of Christendom present far more resemblances of structure than differences. Each maintains the dominical Sacraments. Each has liturgical forms of worship, the so-called free churches maintaining their ascetic worship rubrics with little less strictness than do those of the catholic tradition. Even the ministry is maintained in each church in similar fashion. Each is a little catholicism, succession and continuity carefully preserved. The differences lie in the answers to "succeeding *whom*?" and "continuing *what*?"

In this matter of succession and continuity, this crucial issue in contemporary ecumenical debate, we encounter a curious state of affairs. The Christian Church, divided though it be, does not present us, on the one hand with a church order guarding a succession, and, on the other hand, with church orders lacking ministerial successions. We have, instead, a congeries of successions—episcopal, presbyteral, older, younger. Some of these recognize one another. Others do not. Some give to the fact of succession dogmatic meaning. Others apparently do not. But within a normal Christian communion, the ordaining act is by ministers who themselves have been ordained in a succession. A commission is handed on—a commission which traces back, functionally at least, to the ministerial order or orders of the apostolic age. "Take thou authority . . ." and "Receive the Holy Spirit for the office of . . ." are still the normal ordaining formulae in all Christian communions.

A further fact should be noted. The chief symbol of disunity in the Body of Christ has been a break in a ministerial succession. Anglicans are fond of quoting St. Cyprian's characterization of the episcopate as the "glue" of the church. The metaphor, however, applies to any ministerial succession. The origin of a new denomination may have many causes—clashes of conviction in doctrine or discipline or cult—but such differences do not break outward unity until rival ministerial successions confront each other.

We may have great difficulty in giving doctrinal meaning to ministerial succession in the Church's life, above all to one form of succession as over against another. But it is simply a stubborn fact of history that unity within the Body of Christ, or within fractions of the whole Body, has been dependent upon ministerial continuity. To a representative of the catholic theory of the ministry it is something of an amazing fact that Protestant churches seem to pay so little attention to the doctrine of the ministry, especially the problem of continuity. But the practice of the churches belies the impression of indifference. It would be hard to find a communion, even among those most recently on the historical scene, which does not in practice, deal with its ordination procedures, including the guarding of a succession, very seriously indeed. Would it be ungenerous to ask the question: "Why?"

Ministerial continuity, one should emphasize, insures only one unity in a Church—unity of *Body*. In the famous unity chapter of the Epistle to the Ephesians (f:4-6), seven unities are prescribed

135

for the Church: the unities of body, of the Spirit, of hope, of Christ's Lordship, of faith, of baptism, and finally of the "One God and Father of all." We may note however, that *Body* comes first. It need not be accorded first rank in line of ultimate importance. Even within a broken Body, salvation is possible. Indeed, even to a broken Body of Christ could be applied the phrase: *Extra ecclesiam nulla salus.* Body is not the Spirit. Body can revolt against the Spirit. A body can turn into a corpse. But the author of Ephesians may, despite all these considerations, nevertheless be right in giving unity of Body priority.

The setting, however, in which unity of the Body is given priority needs careful examination. We may note at once that in the list of seven-fold unities of the Ephesian text, the unity of "One Spirit" comes next.

We meet here the issue which, in the view of the present writer, is the crux of the doctrine of the Church as our ecumenical era at least must deal with it. We can call it the Body-Spirit paradox.

The Continental Reformation revolted against a divinization of the institutional Church. The institution, in the Reformer's view, had become an idol. Salvation, so the Reformers proclaimed, consisted in a personal relationship with God, not with a mere hierarchy and sacramental system. Furthermore, they took the adjective "Apostolic" in the Creeds seriously. Continuity of faith was for them a mark of unity in the Church more important than unity of Body. Who will say that they were entirely wrong? Scripture, not tradition, must be primary authority in the Church to preserve apostolic succession in the area of faith. Later history is validating this insight. The Roman Church, as it embraces one novelty of dogma after another, furnishes proof that continuity of hierarchical structure does not guarantee continuity of faith.

Justification by faith became the Reformation war cry. Seen in the light of this doctrine, "the Church must be thought of primarily in terms of the relationship with God for which the doctrine stands. The Reformers therefore defined the Church primarily by reference to grace and faith, not (as 'catholicism' did) by reference to institutional continuity. The Church in its deepest sense is the community of the elect or of those who have saving faith in Christ.

136

The saving relationship of men with God is the result of the divine offer of the gospel, which is conveyed to men by preaching and the sacraments. The necessary marks of the true visible Church are therefore the means of grace, the ministry of word and sacraments." *

So far, so good. Anglicanism, too, made this Reformation insight its own. The only doctrinal definition of the Church found in the Thirty-nine Articles echoes the classic Reformation formula: "The visible Church of Christ is a congregation of faithful men, in which the pure Word of God is preached, and the Sacraments be duly ministered."

But where does this conclusion leave us? Does it solve more than one or two of the great problems surrounding the doctrine of the Church? The Reformation insight need not be minimized. It recalled us to the fact that the *esse* of the New Covenant in Christ, which he wrought and left us as his testament or legacy, is a personal relationship with God the Father through Jesus Christ, in the Fellowship of the Holy Spirit. A substitution of a sacramental system or hierarchically ruled institution for this personal relationship the Reformers called idolatry.

But dangers lurked in this recovery of a lost truth. Does "personal" mean "individualist"—every man for himself? It may be doubted that responsible Protestant theologians have ever pushed the revolt against mediaeval institutionalism to this extreme. Yet it has taken deep root in popular understanding. The emphasis placed in Protestant apologetic upon the doctrine of "the priesthood of all believers" contributed to a deep-going misconception. The fundamental priesthood of the Church is, in the New Testament, clearly the priesthood of the whole Body, or of Christ himself in the Body. The doctrine of the priesthood of the laity "does not mean that laymen are individually priests, but that the laity are, as such, members of that Body which is in its entirety priestly." ** As representative of the Body, the individual layman like the individual priest, each in his special vocation, exercises of course, a priestly ministry.

---

* *The Fulness of Christ*, pp. 30-32
** *Doctrine in the Church of England* (New York: The Macmillan Co., 1938) p. 157.

The Body-Spirit paradox of the Church is not easy of solution.

In the view of the present writer, the solution, if it can be even tentatively discovered, will lie in exploring the full implications of Christian experience. We have this not only in the record of the life of the New Testament *ecclesia*, but also in nigh two thousand years of Church history.

To be a Christian has surely meant, from the very beginning, to enter into new relationship with God. It is not accidental that the book containing the Gospel message is called the New Testament, or New Covenant. This new relationship was made possible by the atoning act of Christ on the Cross. The event which made this new relationship possible must, therefore, first of all be proclaimed. The ministry of the Word, accordingly in chronological sequence, assumes prior importance. "How then shall they call on him in whom they have not believed, and how shall they believe in him of whom they have not heard?" (Romans 10:14). All Christians can agree on a partial definition of the Church as the locus of the proclamation of the Gospel. Even Rome still sends proclaimers of the Gospel into missionary lands as its first ambassadors.

But hearing the Gospel and even believing it to be a proclamation of a true event in the past does not yet make a man a Christian. He must enter into the saving covenant thus proclaimed.

And where is this relationship actualized in history? In the Church—and nowhere else. The reason for this apparent exclusiveness of salvation is, if we take the New Testament story seriously, very simple. It is so simple that it has come, in recent generations, to be frequently ignored.

The classic formula for describing the new relationship with God proclaimed in the Gospel is "through Jesus Christ our Lord." But this Christ through whom we are to enter the new covenant of salvation is no longer here! He was once rabbi, teacher, leader, Messiah, and gathered about himself a group of disciples, But the end of that personal relationship was a crucifixion and a burial.

Christianity did not begin its life in history until a further series of events had taken place—a Resurrection, an Ascension, and, most important of all for the future, a Day of Pentecost, the coming of the Holy Spirit.

The importance of a doctrine of the Holy Spirit for an understanding of the Church cannot be exaggerated. It is the neglect of the doctrine of the Holy Spirit in Christian history which may account for many of our present ecumenical difficulties. But the New Testament record is plain enough. The Third Person of the Trinity is determinative now in the life of the continuing disciple-fellowship. "It is expedient for you that I go away; for if I go not away, the Comforter will not come to you: but if I go, I will send him unto you" (John 16:7). The Holy Spirit, in these words, becomes the representative of Jesus in his Church after his Ascension and until as Christ he appears again as judge of quick and dead. A relationship with Jesus such as the disciples once enjoyed when the Word made flesh is no longer possible. It is of some significance that the word discipleship, or the name for Christ of "Master," do not appear in the epistles of the New Testament, the documents which are normative for a picture of the early Church. Disciples had become Christian—apostles, witnesses, martyrs. The decisive event which, after the Resurrection and Ascension, marked the new aeon or age was the coming of the Comforter.

A recent explorer of the doctrine of the Church in the New Testament paints the contrast between the pre-Pentecostal events of the Gospel story and those which followed in plain words: "We are inclined to establish this difference between the coming of Christ and the coming of the Spirit, that the first is manifest and the second is hidden. Such is not original Christian thinking. According to apostolic language, it is Christ who hides after He accomplished His work here on earth and it is the Spirit who is made manifest. The Spirit is the true theophany after Christ's ascension till the Lord returns again from heaven in the Glory of the Father." *

A further fact must be noted before the New Testament portrayal is complete. The locus of the Holy Spirit is the Church. The Church, in turn, is the Fellowship of the Holy Spirit.

Many puzzles surround the doctrine of the Spirit, even when we limit ourselves to Scripture. We cannot exclude the idea of a

---

* Vonier, Dom Anscar, *The Spirit and the Bride*, Burns Oates, 1935, p. 14.

universal operation of the Holy Spirit in nature and human history. But the evidence is clear that in the picture we get of the Pentecostal gift in Acts and in the writings of St. Paul this gift—by whatever name this new emergence in history is designated—is limited to those who belong to Christ's Body, the Church. The Fourth Gospel, written, we assume, during a late first century decade, declares that during the ministry of Jesus on earth "the Spirit was not yet given; because Jesus was not yet glorified" (John 7:39). The delicacies of trinitarian nomenclature may have bothered the early Church as they still bother us today. Since all three Persons of the Trinity are clearly "holy" and "spiritual," confusion easily resulted when the unique Pentecostal divine presence was given the name Holy Spirit. This difficulty may have induced the author of St. John's Gospel to employ a variant nomenclature. Holy Spirit becomes Advocate or Comforter. A modern scholar goes so far as to suggest that the term "Holy Spirit" is really inadequate to describe or define what the New Testament Church meant by it.*

Turning to the New Testament records, however, just as they stand, one fact must remain undisputed. The Holy Spirit is represented as a gift of "Christ-present" given exclusively to a visible society, and to individuals only as they became members of this society. The exclusive gateway to the reception of the gift was baptism in the name of the Lord Jesus. To become a Christian meant far more than an intellectual acceptance of the historical truth of a past event, or even a loyalty oath to Christianity's Founder, or imitation of his moral perfection. It meant incorporation into a corporate visible body where Christ now was a continuing life and power. A Christian, according to St. Paul, is not one who is individually attached to Christ as a mere follower or disciple. Such a relationship was once possible, though it resulted in the treachery and desertion of those who enjoyed the privilege, but is now superseded by a union with the Lord through his Body, the Church. St. Paul describes this union in the oft repeated definition of Christians as those who are "in Christ." Mysterious as the

---

* Erich Seeberg, *Christliche Dogmatik*, Leipzig, 1925, vol. 2, page 331.

phrase may be, it describes an experience shared by Christians from the days of Pentecost to our own.

Life in the Fellowship of the Holy Spirit is life "in Christ." The "life" of Christ could once be equated with the biography of Jesus on the earthly scene. But the life of Christ in that sense is ended. His continuing "life" is that of the Comforter in the Church. As a contemporary New Testament scholar puts it: "The words 'the life of Christ' mean for us the career of Jesus of Nazareth, but for Paul they would have meant something quite different— the present reality and lordship of the risen one. So, indeed, he actually uses an equivalent phrase in Romans 5:10: 'For if while we were enemies we were reconciled to God by the death of his Son, much more now that we are reconciled, shall we be saved by his life.' The 'life of Christ' is not the remembered life that preceded his death, but the life which followed it—the present life of the Son of God."**

The Holy Spirit, we must conclude, therefore, is this present life of Christ manifested in the Church. If we recall the further fact that the Holy Spirit is first of all a corporate gift or possession, given to an individual only as he is a member of the Fellowship and participates in its life, some light surely is thrown upon the Body— Spirit Paradox of the Church.

The doctrine of the Holy Spirit in the history of Christian thought, as already noted, is puzzling and confused. But Christian experience may well be less confused than the rationalizations of the learned doctors. Spirit—in a modern version of the New Testament often uncapitalized—is not alien to human experience, particularly if we limit the search for analogies to spirit-phenomena in corporate manifestations. The Holy Spirit has many "spiritual" rivals. St. Paul speaks of "the spirit that is now at work in the sons of disobedience" (Eph. 2:2) and of "spiritual wickedness in high places" (Eph. 6:12).

"Believe not every Spirit, but prove the spirits," says St. John (I John 4:1). When St. Paul speaks of "principalities and powers in the heavenly places" (Eph. 3:10), and reminds Christians that their wrestling is against these rather than against mere "flesh

---

** John Knox, *Chapters in a Life of Paul*—Abingdon-Cokesbury, 1950, page 130.

and blood" (Eph. 6:12), he evidently has similar spirit-forces in mind. What are "principalities and powers"? What is a "spirit at work in the sons of disobedience"? These designations must refer to the forces which manifest themselves in any or all human groupings. We still speak of national states as "powers." We speak of the "spirit of America," or the "spirit of a school" or of a city or a club.

Imagination was, in New Testament times, easily led to localize and personalize such experienced forces. They became angels with wings, their abode in "the heavenlies," or in the air which hovers over the geographical home of the group. When we today speak of the spirit of a school, and should ask "where is it?", we might find no better concrete symbolization ready to hand.

The French phrase "espirit de corps" furnishes an analogy rich in possibilities. A grouping, a "body," is ruled over by a "spirit." This spirit is the uniting power within the group. It does not exist in the individual as such. It lives in relationship, between the persons who compose the body. As a recent explorer of spirit in community life asserts: "only through entering into relation can man live in the spirit." *

The term "body" has appeared in the exploration of the above analogy as an inevitable word. Spirit without body is, on our earthly scene, inconceivable. Furthermore, spirit, to be enabled to exercise "spiritual" power, requires a united body—united by a common faith, but also by a physical oneness. Every group, if it wishes to live by enspiriting powers, sacredly guards sacramental symbols of unity—an entrance sacrament first of all.

No one can have the gifts—be they for good or for evil—of "esprit de corps" except by membership in the "corps." Then its "esprit" is his for the asking. The spirit which empowers the group, and which is its "soul," will then mould the individual to the life-pattern of the group, will impart power and many another grace. It imparts worth and status and function.

Turning back now to the Body-Spirit paradox of the Church, and applying, with safeguards against literalizing in mind, the analogy of spirit as corporate power, can we see meaning in the

* J. H. Oldham, *Real Life is Meeting,* the Sheldon Press, London, 1942, p. 32.

apparently presumptuous claim: *Extra ecclesiam nulla salus?*
When a pagan in the days of the early Church became a Christian,
he had to make an individual decision, of course. But the decisive
act was not merely believing the Gospel proclamation as true,
though that would be involved in the total event. Nor was it merely what we have come to call deciding for Christ or accepting
Christ as ethical model. He knew himself to require rescue from
the demonic principalities and powers which held sovereignty over
the pagan society in which he had lived hitherto. The decisive step,
accordingly, was baptism, his being incorporated into the society
ruled over by the Holy Spirit. A Christ-convert relationship some-
how apart from such incorporation would be hard to trace in the
New Testament record.

It is clearly to the credit of the awesome catholicisms of Christendom that they have borne witness through the centuries to
half at least of the Body-Spirit paradox of the Church. Experience
can validate the principle that corporate spirit without corporate
body is an illusion, and that, furthermore, the physical precedes
the spiritual. Without membership in a faith-community actualized in history, no gift of the Holy Spirit, and without Holy Spirit,
no living Christ, and without living Christ, no Church and no
Christians.

But, as pointed out earlier, bodily unity is only one of the unities
demanded of the Church. There are, one must add, various kinds
of unity of body. Is Rome, with her pyramid of hierarchical rule
the kind of Body of Christ pictured in the New Testament? Is this
the Fellowship of the Holy Spirit? The very word "fellowship"
indicts Rome's guardianship of the covenant established by the
Church's Lord. An institution dispensing grace as if it were de-
personalized into things is perverting spiritual power. Spirit requires body. But the body must be a personal fellowship. If Rome,
as the great western Catholicism, has preserved half of the Body-
Spirit paradox of the Church, she has neglected the other half.
More than one historian of doctrine can testify that a doctrine of
the Holy Spirit in terms of a corporate possession and power,
shared with every member, is largely a blank in Rome's scholastic
system. The laity, to cite an obvious proof, are disfranchised.

If we turn, by way of contrast, to the opposite extreme of church-life, we see the Body-Spirit paradox illustrated from the other side. It cannot be an accident that the newest sects arising on Protestant soil bear the generic name "Pentecostal." Ancestral to these are the churches which define their peculiar genius as "congregational," or which practice the corporateness of the "class meeting." Here is rediscovery of the New Testament power of group unity and group "spirit." Sober judgment may question the validity of the fruits of some of the undisciplined spirit-phenomena of the Pentecostal sects. But they cannot but remind the observer of the original Pentecostal flock. The power of prophecy and of witnessing and unfettered prayer, and of mutual brotherliness has once more been poured out on all flesh.

But our Pentecostal communions have not escaped the Body-Spirit paradox. In some respects they illustrate it even more clearly than do the great catholicisms. The institutional church has been transformed into a people-church. But as such it guards its entrance sacrament (often immersion-baptism) as exclusively as does Rome. No individual is the bearer of the group-spirit in isolation. Spirit is "esprit de corps." Individualist liturgical practice or belief means exclusion, or the founding of a rival sect. But within each sectarian boundary, Christ is experienced again as the living Lord. And this Lord is the Spirit.

All honor to the post-Reformation sects! With all their faults and weaknesses they are in many aspects the rediscovered Church of the New Testament in miniature. Often despised or belittled by the older and more institutionalized Christian communions, they yet can serve as a model whenever a parish, let alone a larger division of a Church, is stirred to live up to the pattern of church life given us in the New Testament. A remarkable rediscovery of what a Christian parish can become when it is again a fellowship of spiritual power, every member, even the humblest layman, sharing in the apostolic ministry of saving souls, is going on even in the Church of Rome. Few more thrilling accounts of such a revival of Church life under New Testament standards can be found today than that contained in the recent book *Revolution in a*

144

City Parish, written by a French Roman Catholic priest.* Such a parish would resemble with limitations, to be sure, yet with striking analogies, the Pentecostal sect. There would be again the full experience of individual Christians becoming members one of another, of forgiving one another and "speaking the truth in love." The great Pauline phrase "in Christ" would take on vivid meaning. Christ himself would be in the midst of the flock—as Holy Spirit, as the power of the new relationship of love (agape) which unites the members with their One Lord, and with one another in One Faith. The Body-Spirit paradox, in parish manifestation, would be resolved.

The Pentecostal sect, however, as, indeed, sectarianism and denominationalism generally, stands under awesome judgment. "Is Christ divided?" (I Cor. 1:13). If the New Testament gives us a portrayal of each Church congregation as a Spirit-bearing body, it also insists on unity as between the scattered flocks. We meet "the Church of God in Corinth," for example, as a manifestation locally of the covenant in Christ which embraces all members everywhere. Divisions, if permitted at all, were geographical, not denominational. To see four church spires on a city square, rivals for membership (clearly a crucial symptom), would have shocked St. Paul. Even intercommunion between the separated flocks would not have met the demand for unity. To be "members one of another" (Eph. 4:25) means more than this. It means being incorporated into one Body, united by "bodily" unifying structural forms and sacraments. And—unpalatable as the fact may be for denominational ease of conscience—the one unvarying structural means of "bodily" oneness in the history of the churches in ministerial succession!

The word succession involves the problem of continuity. The unity of Christ's people must be one in time as well as space. We are all to meet as one flock under one Shepherd in the Church triumphant. The Pentecostal sect may illustrate the richness of meaning in the definition of the Church as a Fellowship of the Holy Spirit. But what about the equally demanding definition of the Church as the Communion of Saints? Are our fathers in the

---

* Abbe Michonneau, *Revolution in a City Parish,* Newman Press, Westminster, Md. 1950.

Faith to be disfranchised or our brother disinherited? Such a break in fellowship may not always be overt and intentional, yet is not this one of the things that actually takes place when a new sect emerges in history? How much of a feeling of fellowship, to cite a possibly embarrassing example, does a Methodist rejoice in with regard to his forefathers in a now rival communion in comparison with that which he enjoys with the remembered saints of his own communion from the days of John Wesley to the present? As argued earlier in this essay, a profound valuation of the continuity of the Church of Christ is not limited to Catholicism. Even the most recent sectarian flock requires only a very few years of existence before it venerates its founding fathers, its emerging liturgical traditions, its unity in time as well as the unifying bonds between geographically separated congregations. Every sect discovers for itself that it is a Communion of Saints, communion including past members as well as present. The difference between a post-Reformation sect or denomination and the churches in the Catholic tradition is different not nearly so much of basic structure or form as in relative continuity of on-going life and form and structure. Each, if it were without rival on the historical scene, would reduplicate much of the development of Catholicism, tradition taking its place alongside Scripture as at least auxiliary authority, and a ministry developing hierarchical gradations analogous to episcopal polity, a papacy itself, with a Vatican, not entirely impossible.

The writer of this essay is an Anglican. The reader may long have been under the suspicion that the final resultant of the essay's argument will be a presentation of the historic episcopate. A plea of "guilty" is justified. If the Body-Spirit paradox is basic to a doctrine of the Church as we, in our era of ecumenical striving, must struggle with it; if, further, Christian experience proves, within post-Reformation communions as well as in the great Catholicisms, that unity of Spirit involves unity of Body; if unity of Body is one which cannot bypass the unity of the Communion of Saints throughout all the centuries of Christian faith and life; if, by accident of history or the guidance of the Holy Spirit, ministerial succession is, in all communions, the chief sacramental means and

146

symbol of structural unity, in time and space—then clearly, the problem of which succession can best unify the scattered flocks of Christ's Church is not on the periphery of ecumenical concern, but at its very heart.

It is not the purpose of this essay, however, to launch forth at its closing on a full debate on apostolic succession. My object has been rather to show the relevance of the problem of an historic ministry in the Church as a whole and to give it a doctrinal setting. No specific Church structure may be able to prove the right to be the *esse* of the Church of Christ. The marks of the Church which may assert such a right are unity of Body and unity of Spirit, and the right of unity of Body to be a requisite for unity of the Spirit. Acceptance of the further need to do full justice to unity in the Communion of Saints will lead inevitably to rousing ecumenical conscience to deal seriously with the problem of continuity also—continuity which can express sacramentally our unity in Christ with our Christian brethren before the days of the Reformation as well as after, as this will surely be demand as well as privilege when we meet together in the eternal home of the "One God and Father of us all."